SELF OBSERVATION

EXPERIENCES

AND

MENTAL WELLNESS

CHUKWUMA EMUWA

SELF OBSERVATION: EXPERIENCES AND MENTAL WELLNESS

Published by Topdale Books Limited
ISBN 978-978-771-881-0 (Paperback)
ISBN 978-978-771-882-7 (EBook)

ACKNOWLEDGMENT

I thank God for giving me the strength and opportunity to finish this book. I dedicate this book to my parents. The traumatic experience of my father's demise serves as the motivation for this publication.

Furthermore, I observed a decline in visits from many individuals my father assisted after his passing. You can say, they literally disappeared after his death. Nonetheless, it is part of life to be open to any experience - good or bad. I am deeply grateful for my mother's remarkable fortitude and resilience despite the challenges we faced.

I hereby acknowledge the staff members of the following for their efforts in making this book possible: Nnamdi Azikiwe Library, University of Nigeria (Nsukka), National Library (Lagos), Herbert Macaulay Library (Lagos), American Corner (U.S Embassy) Lagos, Kenneth Dike Library (Anambra), CambaBooks, and Topdale Books.

I appreciate the Christian Broadcasting Network, and The 700 Club for their words of inspiration and prayers.

TABLE OF CONTENTS

CHAPTER TWO: 70
IMPACT OF STRESS AT DIFFERENT LIFE STAGES

CHAPTER THREE: 82
EMOTIONS AS SIGNALS

PREFACE

Navigating my thoughts, feelings and emotions as an adult is way more challenging than I imagined. Overthinking, and trying to make sense of what is happening in my inner life is so exhausting!

The traumatic experience started following the death of my father during a surgical operation to remove a ruptured appendix. My mother - who was a primary school teacher - had five young children (between the ages of 11-18) to cater for. Being the youngest in the family, I reckoned that things would not be the same anymore; I couldn't process all that was going on. I deeply sympathised with my mum during those difficult times.

Gradually, I became super cautious to avoid making errors or getting hurt. During a football game, I collided with someone, and I felt pain in my thigh. I feared a broken bone and potential infection. Our family doctor, an orthopaedic surgeon, reassured me that it wasn't serious and that the pain would subside soon. I quit playing football owing to that experience. A nagging fear of getting infected propelled me to adopt frequent hand washing, especially after physical contact or touching surfaces. My siblings teased me, but

I couldn't shake off the fear of falling ill from one of the numerous diseases I had heard about. Thus, with an utmost sense of commitment and dedication, I was resolute in my decision to maintain a hygienic lifestyle despite being low-risk.

Living with my uncle revealed the harsh reality that empathy is often lacking in some families. As a teenager, I questioned whether he was, in fact, my father's brother. I witnessed my uncle speaking terribly of all his siblings and his relations in their absence. He exhibited harshness, extending to inadequate nutritious meals. We relied on monetary assistance from our mother, enabling us to purchase essentials at our uncle's residence or dine at nearby relatives' homes, whenever there was such an opportunity. Those days were tough for me due to the challenges I encountered. In response to my grievances, I consistently received assurances that the difficulties would be temporary with statements like, "Do manage; it will soon be over." I became really withdrawn and sad, so much so that the cumulative effect led to an increasing contemplation of abandoning my family and everyone to go start life in a faraway place.

The first step I took was to cease feigning normalcy within the household. Conversation with my uncle was limited to "bring this or that" or 'go to this place or that place.' In the presence of visitors, my uncle presented a jovial facade, feigning warmth and friendship with us. In response to his attempts at humour, I began to openly display my sorrow. My uncle was taken aback when I started expressing my genuine emotions, and our guests promptly understood the situation. Upon exposing the truth, the pretence ceased. Nevertheless, he redirected his wrath towards me.

Upon commencing my undergraduate studies, I knew I couldn't keep up with those stresses. I notified my uncle and siblings about my struggles. My love for reading fostered my knowledge of the profession and practices of therapists. In our environment at that time, access to professional therapy was unavailable. Mental health issues were stigmatised. Anyone with mental health issues was viewed either as someone cursed, insane, or having a spiritual attack!

I was a straight-A student excelling in sciences and arts, thus emerging as one of the best students in these fields. Despite the challenges I was battling, I was the overall best student in many categories. My outward appearance led others to assume that I was trouble-free, fortunate, and well-behaved. To my dismay, after I notified my uncle and siblings, nothing came out of it. So, I had to go and see a doctor to explain my challenges and why I was having difficulties focusing on my academics. My primary focus of study was on biography and psychology and I was driven by a desire to understand life better and improve myself. Following consultations with multiple medical professionals, I received diagnoses ranging from potential cerebral malaria to myopia requiring corrective eyewear. I felt embarrassed and ashamed of the situation I found myself in. My circumstances led some to perceive me as lacking seriousness, prompting introspection and existential questioning. "Why is this happening to me? Why is God allowing me to go through this? I am not a bad person?" Why me?" I often soliloquised.

In the absence of anticipated empathy and support, I assumed my family was ignorant of the situation. I felt ashamed but also relieved that I had finally told them. Out of empathy, I spared my mother additional stress, given her effort to supplement our uncle's support. I withdrew further, knowing I was in the battle alone. Thenceforth I encountered so many challenges that significantly impacted my educational pursuits that I tried to run away to another country.

I also intensified efforts to learn more about life and the situations I found myself in. My family never revisited or acknowledged the challenges I shared; they acted like I never told them. Therefore, I concentrated on addressing my personal struggles, trusting that God will bring a miracle. Stress, phobias, insomnia, and anxieties are all part of my life. A prolonged learning process and experimentation enabled me to comprehend the underlying factors contributing to my lifelong struggles, spanning childhood, adolescence, and adulthood. The combination of poor coping skills, lack of preparedness and inadequate support significantly extended my period of suffering. Putting the pieces of my life together was difficult, but with determination and strong faith in God, I got out of the lonely path. I achieved a state of complete presence, peaceful mind with a sense of what is within, and beyond my control. My journey was a prolonged learning process that highlighted the importance of early skill acquisition.

Early development of adaptive coping skills and appreciation for life's pleasures is vital. Empowering children and young teenagers with essential life skills prepares them for future challenges - just like the way we teach children how to read, write, and eat. Equipping these young ones with critical thinking, life understanding and coping skills helps prepare them for the unforeseen.

INTRODUCTION

We are meant to embrace challenges and enjoy life by intentionally living a life of purpose and meaning, constantly immersed in doing the right things with proper knowledge whilst focusing on the present moment. We cannot change the world, situations, or events, but we can change how we react. Thus, we must understand our underlying beliefs, rules, and patterns holistically. A unified mind-body-spirit approach, rooted in core values and principles, fosters resilience, purpose, and peak performance. So, when our behaviour is not in harmony with our spirit, we experience stress. A comprehensive grasp of how to effectively regulate, and guide our emotions, thoughts, and behaviour is expedient for optimal functioning, and overall well-being. Ignoring this has the potential to negatively affect us and the lives of people we meet.

There are different experiences we encounter in life - be it as a child, student, parent, friend, father, etc. Our appreciation of life's experiences is contingent upon recognising the distinction between our true essence, and temporary circumstances, thereby avoiding attachment-induced suffering. We must enjoy each experience fully and move on without regret or loss. Cultivating non-attachment to people, places, things, and experiences is crucial in life. Detaching from people, places, things, and experiences is expedient as they do not define us. Life's meaning goes beyond achievement, degrees, spouses, children, and events.

We grow by letting go and exploring within. Regrettably, numerous individuals internalise flawed ideologies and misconceptions, leading to distorted perceptions and an undue emphasis on material possessions, relationships, and social status. Individuals who tie their identity to external entities are predisposed to significant emotional distress when faced with loss or potential threats to these attachments. It can precipitate persistent emotional turmoil, characterised by fear, worry, anxiety, depression, and self-destructive behaviours, in an attempt to protect and control things they ought not to.

Children involuntarily internalise their parents' perspectives, which become deeply ingrained in their subconscious. Hence parental biases can sneak into a child's subconscious and have a ripple effect on their behavioural pattern.

Human behaviour is shaped significantly by unconscious factors, but mindfulness practices enable conscious awareness and intentional thought. Mindfulness enables conscious observation of thoughts, facilitating self-awareness and discernment of healthy versus unhealthy thought patterns. Thus, we can switch from negative, unhealthy thought patterns to positive/healthy ones, and make it a habit. Releasing negativity unlocks our true potential, aligning us with life's purpose.

The mind's purpose is to generate thoughts, but we can choose which thoughts to pursue or dismiss. We need to pay attention to thoughts that arise and our emotions. In times of action, we are guided by our core values, morals, and deeply held beliefs. In that state of observation, our mind achieves a mode of serenity and quietness, allowing thoughts to arise without attachment or distraction. In that state, we are calm, focused, peaceful, and fully present in the moment.

This book offers valuable insights and practical guidance for individuals of all ages. Its primary objective is to empower children and young teenagers with essential life skills and knowledge, providing a solid foundation for navigating life's challenges. This comprehensive resource is divided into five distinct parts:

Chapter 1 focuses on pivotal life experiences and their profound impact on cognitive processes, emotional responses, and behavioural patterns. This chapter also provides insightful guidance on recognizing and managing significant life experiences, fostering heightened self-awareness and effective coping strategies.

Chapter 2 focuses on how stress affects us at different stages of life (childhood, adolescence, adulthood, and old age).

Chapter 3 focuses on some emotions and their signs.

Chapter 4 focuses on self-destructive behaviour and suicide.

Chapter 5 focuses on self-care, empowering readers to prioritise their well-being, and optimise their ability to tackle life's obstacles.

EXPERIENCES AND MENTAL HEALTH OUTCOMES

PARENTING

Children rely on parents for security, nurturing, and guidance. Children learn right from wrong, and adaptive coping mechanisms through observational learning from their parents. Children learn fast from parents with strong coping mechanisms and adaptive behaviour. Parents' bad behaviours can impact children's self-esteem and development. Parenting styles significantly influence child development outcomes during this critical growth phase. Parents employ diverse parenting styles, often influenced by intergenerational transmission of practices, adult experiences, and peer influences.

Controlling parents demand absolute compliance, often disregarding children's opinions; they are emotionally distant. Also, controlling parents readily criticise and discipline children for non-compliance, neglecting to offer explanatory reasoning. Children in controlling households often struggle with self-doubt, exhibiting low self-esteem and uncertainty; they experience diminished self-worth and impaired social abilities. Children trapped in controlling environments may rebel as a means of escape while lacking effective coping skills.

Understanding parents engage in active listening to comprehend their children and help them to be independent and guide their children's exploratory endeavours. They create loving boundaries, promote healthy living, and regulate emotions and behaviour. Children in such environments are more likely to have enhanced social skills and good mental health. Children raised in supportive environments typically excel academically and exhibit high self-esteem and confidence in their parents (a manifestation of a strong parent-child relationship).

Indulgent parents adopt a permissive approach, characterised by minimal expectations, lenient boundaries, and excessive indulgence, providing ample freedom and relaxed guidance while minimising demands and responsibilities. Children raised in indulgent environments become 'spoiled brats' as they become selfish and lazy; always needing Mum and Dad.

Uninvolved parents exhibit indifference. They maintain emotional distance and fail to establish clear expectations or responsibilities. Basic needs are met, but emotional support and attachment are absent. Children raised in such an environment often struggle with self-esteem and confidence, they might search for love and validation elsewhere because they are not getting it at home.

SUGGESTIONS:

Parenting styles vary, and what works for one family may not work for another. Factors influencing parenting style are also dependent on circumstances. Parents often blend elements from multiple styles to create a unique approach tailored to their family's needs. For example, parents facing challenges like long work hours to make ends meet may struggle with being available for their children. Children's needs and the family's size significantly impact parenting styles. Environment and cultural expectations play a prominent role. Child behaviour and temperament significantly influence parenting style, as well as parental upbringing and experiences.

PARENTAL PRESSURE

Parents want the best for their children, they aspire for their children to achieve excellence across various disciplines. Parents desire their children's overall well-being, social harmony, and distinguished achievements. While parental expectations may stem from good intentions, parents frequently project their own aspirations, values, and unfinished goals onto their children. These expectations drive parental enforcement mechanisms, leading to undue stress on the children.

Parents raised under uninvolved parenting styles may overcompensate through excessive expectations. Unmet expectations prompt verbal rebukes, criticisms, and shouting. Some parents may continually remind their children of their sacrifices and expectations while emphasising the importance of justifying their investment. Excessive parental expectations can provoke rebellion in children. Children who fail to meet unrealistic expectations may experience severe emotional distress, leading to depression, negative self-talk and self-criticism, delinquency, and aggression. They may experience social isolation, friendship difficulties, and estrangement from their parents. Weight-related pressure can contribute to the development of eating disorders. Those pressured into marriages for social status or parental approval may exhibit rebellious backlash. They may enter the marriage to avoid unnecessary stress and punitive action from their parents.

SUGGESTIONS:

Parents should refrain from completing their child's assignments to ensure academic integrity. Parents should engage their children in conversations while encouraging them to develop problem-solving skills. Rather than promoting weight concerns, they should prioritise healthy habits. Children need to understand that their parents also have their 'fair share' of pressure, challenges, and experiences. They should strive to comprehend parental actions, and not take it too personally.

Though not an easy feat, learning effective coping skills will be helpful. Developing coping skills enables children to navigate parental expectations effectively. This approach mitigates potential negative impacts on their mental health.

DOMESTIC ABUSE

Healthy relationships exclude all forms of domestic violence. A fulfilling relationship requires emotional maturity whereby they can understand and manage their emotions, feelings, and behaviour. However, real-life relationships are not perfect, they tag along with their own frictions. How partners handle issues, and their mental health will decide the outcome.

Some instances of abuse:

Abuse can involve forced control over a partner's actions, access to phone, finances, etc. Partners often display jealousy and suspicion.

Physical assaulting the other partner.

Threatening or restricting partner's social interactions, controlling who they see or talk to, not letting them go out.

In some instances, one partner tries to isolate the other from friends and family.

EFFECTS OF ABUSE

Domestic abuse has long-lasting effects on the family. It has a profound impact on victims and their children, causing both immediate and lasting harm. Children exposed to domestic violence within their family unit are likely to experience profound, far-reaching, and diverse consequences, affecting their emotional, psychological, behavioural and social development. Some may have trouble sleeping. Children exposed to domestic violence may experience significant declines in academic achievement. Children may feel guilty or responsible for their parent's struggles. Physical symptoms like headaches and stomach issues may arise.

For Teenagers:

Some may develop low self-esteem. They may struggle to make friends and engage in risky behaviours. They will need help in school and may be prone to anxiety and depression. They may become an ally of one parent. They may mimic aggressive behaviour or bully others based on the violence they witness at the home front. Their self-esteem will be impacted, and some may develop eating disorders.

For The Abused:

Traumatic experiences (in the event of an assault) can lead to PTSD, anxiety, and depression. They may feel hopeless and confined.

There may be a lack of trust in the family and the relationship may end in divorce or separation.

SUGGESTIONS:

Children exposed to domestic violence require targeted counselling to alleviate self-blame and guilt.

One of the partners in the relationship must prioritise children's safety. Couple therapy is essential.

Aggressive partners need treatment and anger management therapy.

In situations where loss of life needs to be prevented, dissolution of the relationship may be the most viable solution.

MANIPULATION

This is a deliberate attempt to shape someone's behaviour, often covertly, to serve one's own interest. Manipulators use multiple strategies to achieve their goals. Parents may manipulate children to obey or turn against their partner, and some older siblings might adopt the same measure to control their younger ones. Unhealthy manipulation involves coercive tactics, and disregarding emotional harm.

Some tactics involve exploiting confidential information shared with them to manipulate individuals into compliance. Other manipulative tactics include dishonesty and denial, to distort reality and undermine the victim's perception. They may employ condescending and mocking behaviour, often disguised as playful teasing, to undermine the confidence of their victims. They blame others for their mistakes to avoid accountability. They can blackmail and sabotage their victim's reputation, exposing them to vulnerability. They strategically foster discord among loved ones, facilitating covert manipulation. Manipulation fosters an environment of distrust, eroding self-confidence, and self-worth, and it causes communication problems.

SUGGESTIONS:

To prevent manipulation, it is important to exercise discretion when sharing information with others, including intimate partners and friends. This ensures that nobody isolates you from family or friends. It is necessary to establish healthy boundaries with manipulative individuals through strategic contact limitation. One should share information with a witness present to prevent denial or misrepresentation.

Seek support if one partner exhibits manipulative behaviour due to upbringing, as this might be a coping mechanism for dealing with an unhealthy life.

SINGLE PARENTHOOD

Single Parenthood stems from divorce, separation, and other factors. Additionally, unforeseen life events, such as out-of-wedlock births or personal choices lead to single parenthood. Advances in reproductive technology enable unmarried individuals, including women and men, to opt for solo parenthood through assisted reproduction methods like IVF.

Irrespective of the options, a child nurtured in a stable, supportive environment with effective coping strategies will thrive and reach their full potential. In instances of divorce or separation, children may experience developmental implications, influencing their emotional, social, and psychological growth. The exception occurs when parents establish a mutually respectful and collaborative co-parenting arrangement, prioritising the child's comfort and well-being. Children can spend time with both parents without unnecessary stress and quarrels.

Children thrive with increased responsibility and emotional connection when living with one parent in a supportive environment. Prolonged parental conflict over visitation, custody, and child support can have detrimental effects on children's emotional and psychological well-being, and their grades may suffer. Children from economically stressed households, where parents are preoccupied with financial pressures, thereby not paying attention to their welfare, face an increased risk of academic disengagement and dropout. Seeing the differences between themselves and others, children's mental well-being may be affected.

Children from dysfunctional or economically stressed households face increased vulnerability to substance abuse and self-harm due to heightened emotional distress. Some single parents from divorced backgrounds may employ manipulative tactics to influence their children's perceptions, fostering negative emotions and animosity towards the other parent. Children gradually turn against the targeted parent based on manipulative tactics and false information.

Ensuring that the child is safe and well-supported in a nurturing environment is essential.

SUGGESTIONS:
Establishing and maintaining a consistent daily schedule, incorporating essential activities such as nutrition, physical activity, and sleep is important.

Parents should use emotional support and stress management strategies to mitigate potential harm to their children.

FAVOURITISM

Favouring one child causes friction in the family. Lack of awareness of this among some parents may significantly impact their children. Parental support and encouragement significantly contribute to children's positive self-esteem, confidence, and overall well-being. Disproportionate attention is sometimes given to younger or male children, or biological offspring compared to step/foster children.

Some of the consequences of favouritism include fuelling sibling rivalry. The less favoured children become unhappy about being ignored, potentially leading to harmful behaviour towards the favoured siblings. Favouritism erodes self-esteem in the less favoured children.

Favouritism cultivates an environment of unhealthy competition, potentially leading to bullying. It stifles creativity in unfavoured children. Favoured children develop inflated self-importance and a sense of entitlement. Favouritism fosters pampering and self-centredness, leading to potential strain in the children's relationships.

SUGGESTIONS:

Parents should treat each child equally and avoid taking sides. Parents should establish a clear standard for behaviour and avoid comparing or praising children publicly for exceptional performance. Instead, they should focus on each child's unique needs for support.

SIBLING RIVALRY

Sibling rivalry originating in childhood can perpetuate into adulthood. Children inherently possess a competitive spirit, driven to succeed and excel in various activities, especially winning and being first in games. The way adults and caregivers manage sibling relationships significantly impacts the development of healthy competition.

Parental favouritism, where one child receives disproportionate praise and attention, fosters resentment and rivalry in other siblings. Consequently, children struggle for parental affection. Conflict, jealousy, competition, comparison, and show-off will be evident, and the motive will be to diminish the others' value and make them feel inferior. Children and adults may experience anxiety and loneliness. Childhood sibling rivalry can persist and transform into adult conflicts and disagreements.

SUGGESTIONS:

It is essential for parents to lead by example, ensuring equal treatment for all and avoiding rivalry.

They should avoid being biased in favour of any child or having a favourite child.

They should encourage empathy and teamwork among the children.

Where parental support is insufficient or unavailable, individuals should actively seek and establish a reliable support system.

They should avoid bragging, and ostentatious displays of success or material possessions.

Children should maintain emotional objectivity when faced with parental favouritism toward a successful sibling. They should embrace and recognise the limits of personal influence and relinquish stress over uncontrollable circumstances.

DOMESTIC STAFF ABUSE

Many countries lack robust legal frameworks and institutional safeguards to protect the vulnerable in society. Domestic workers in various homes frequently face a high level of abuse. The exploitation of vulnerable workers persists due to poverty and ignorance. Some employers use coercive tactics to manipulate, discipline and isolate employees. Female employers are often the target of employer sexual abuse. They work in poor conditions with inadequate rest and food. Employers may withhold agreed-upon payment. They can sack employers without providing accrued wages. They are denied adequate rest and subjected to inhumane treatment, effectively reducing them to subhuman status. Workers recognise that authorities often fail to intervene when they report exploitation, as the absence of a formal contract leaves them vulnerable to abuse.

Victims suffer stress, anxiety, and depression, exacerbated by isolation from others. Victims of exploitation may retaliate against their employers, often targeting vulnerable individuals such as children in their care or harming the employer's family. Additionally, some domestic workers face unique challenges stemming from past trauma, including being brought up in dysfunctional environments, which can profoundly impact their behaviour and well-being.

SUGGESTIONS:

A comprehensive law is essential to safeguard the rights of domestic workers globally.

Institutions must prioritise monitoring the well-being of domestic workers in countries plagued by widespread abuse.

People should have empathy towards one another.

INFIDELITY

Infidelity occurs when one partner engages in a sexual or emotional relationship with someone outside the relationship, causing devastating emotional pain to the other partner. This betrayal can lead to anxiety, trust issues, and depression, with lasting negative effects. The situation is inherently stressful, often triggering anger toward the unfaithful partner. Children are also deeply affected, and often experience intense emotional turmoil following parental infidelity, leading to confusion, anxiety, and trust issues.

SUGGESTIONS:

To preserve trust and harmony, partners should prioritise fidelity and avoid infidelity's devastating consequences.

Rather than moving on, and ignoring the effects posed

by infidelity, couples should opt for professional therapy to cope with the situation.

They must put everything in proper perspective and resolve to move on amicably.

PEER PRESSURE

This is pressure from a particular group on an individual to behave in a certain way. The impact can be healthy or unhealthy, depending on the motive behind it. Peer pressure impacts different areas, such as school, neighbourhood, professional organisation, and motherhood.

Indirect peer pressure is the desire to fit in with a particular class/group, driven by a need for acceptance.

It is beneficial when peer pressure is positive, motivating individuals to excel in academics or achieve excellence in their chosen field. However, peer pressure can turn harmful and toxic when it promotes reckless behaviour and unhealthy competition. In children, peer pressure that yields good conduct is excellent, however, peer pressure that yields negativity is not.

Such negatives are:

Taking things that do not belong to them.

Being headstrong.

Dressing in a certain way.

Maintaining their distance in the house.

Children may adopt behaviours that deviate from their parents' values or norms.

In teenagers:

To get attention, they may try to appear different.

They may engage in high-risk behaviours, including reckless sexual activity, substance abuse, and alcohol.

Their academic performance in school will likely be affected.

In adults, positive peer pressure can be beneficial, just as it is in children and teenagers. Positive peer pressure can inspire individuals to make beneficial choices and exhibit good behaviour.

However, negative pressure can lead to unhealthy behaviours. They face intense pressure to conform to specific behaviours and to stand out. Some individuals will be involved in unnecessary comparisons with their neighbours, colleagues, and family members.

This leads to pressure to maintain a certain lifestyle, including:
- Choice of cars.
- Choice of vacations they embark on.
- Choice of groups they mingle with.

They will attempt to exceed their financial capacity to gain acceptance from their peer group, thereby straining their finances.

They will attempt to display their superiority by flaunting their membership in an elite group, separating themselves from those they consider less worthy.

Negative peer pressure is hazardous as it can lead to a lot of stress and anxiety, impacting the person's mental health. The risks of indulging in an unhealthy lifestyle like wild partying, orgies, substance abuse, and stealing, to meet up expectations, are extremely high.

SUGGESTIONS:

The primary objective is to identify and avoid negative influences.

Foster a strong sense of self-esteem, establish and maintain healthy boundaries, and develop assertiveness by learning to say 'No.'

Seek advice from trusted people before joining any group or committing to a particular lifestyle.

Parents need to provide nurturing environments and be emotionally responsive to their needs.

Parents should teach children effective coping mechanisms and emphasise that group affiliation is not mandatory.

WE vs THEM EFFECT

While categorisation itself is not inherently wrong, problems arise when:

1. Groups exclude others.
2. Favouritism or bias occurs.

Leaders may feel that society unfairly puts pressure on them to perform magic in governance.

It is unsurprising that leaders in some countries believe citizens should appreciate their efforts. Citizens, meanwhile, focus on the leaders' luxurious lifestyles. They compare leaders' luxurious lifestyles to their own struggles, criticising excesses, and demanding fiscal responsibility.

Thus, some attack the leadership, saying they are corrupt and insensitive. Ironically, upon assuming leadership roles, some individuals forsake their initial values and adopt the lavish lifestyles and behaviours of their predecessors. This may cause people to doubt the new leader's loyalty.

When someone crosses into leadership, their perspective shifts from citizen to leader. Joining the leadership ranks, he aligns with their mindset. Thus, the 'We vs Them' narrative is anchored on allegiance at a certain period in life.

In a spiritual or religious circle, the same 'We vs Them' mentality persists. The men of God, such as pastors and priests, often elevate themselves above their congregations. In many countries with robust laws, many men of God are held accountable for their excesses. However, some spiritual leaders exploit and control their followers to succumb to their 'imposed will.' Followers' complaints about leadership are often dismissed with biblical quotes emphasising obedience to authority, first. This fosters a hierarchical structure, where leaders are superior, and followers are inferior. As a result, some followers aspire to leadership roles to wield similar power, hence a vicious circle is created. Upon assuming leadership roles, they switch from advocating accountability to 'obey your leader's quotation' style.

Social circles often perpetuate the 'We vs Them' mentality, between the wealthy class and the poor class. So, the wealthy ones may perceive the poor as expecting handouts (thereby seeing them as entitled people) because they look to them for support. Without understanding their peculiar circumstances, the wealthy may label the poor as lazy or needy. Conversely, the poor may view the wealthy as insensitive and not doing enough for society, despite their substantial resources.

Within certain family and social circles, individuals who acquire wealth often compare themselves to childhood friends and siblings. They believe they are now better than them and adopt the attitude of 'we are not on the same level anymore.' This tends to affect relationships among family members and former close friends.

Additionally, wealthy individuals enjoy privileged access to certain places, unavailable to the poor owing to economic disparities. The grouping is not absolute, as individuals can become wealthy, and join the wealthy class. Wealthy individuals can experience misfortunes, leading to loss of privileges, and former social status.

In many other areas, there are also different classifications, like married women vs unmarried. This causes some married women to associate only with fellow married women and avoid getting in touch with their friends who are not yet married.

Racial and ethnic groups sometimes exhibit similar biases, with certain groups considering themselves superior.

The 'We vs Them' mindset is encountered openly or subtly in many areas. The main danger is that people subconsciously use this to treat others in a certain way. While one group enjoys respect and dignity, others face neglect, leading to feelings of isolation. This classification can erode the self-esteem of the neglected group, particularly those lacking robust coping mechanisms.

This classification fosters discrimination and exclusion, denying certain individuals access to activities and experiences.

SUGGESTIONS:
We need to always look for similarities in people instead of differences. We should focus on shared humanity: seeking similarities over differences.

It is essential to minimise distance between people and groups.

Practice empathy.

Let us support and uplift our siblings and community to the best of our abilities.

We need to be mindful of our actions, every step of the way.

NEIGHBOURHOOD

Neighbourhood environments profoundly impact individual mental well-being. A safe and crime-free neighbourhood fosters a stable and supportive environment for children's growth and development. Inequality and poverty significantly contribute to living in unhealthy neighbourhoods. Living in unhealthy neighbourhoods exposes children and teenagers to heightened risks of physical and social disorders, including crime, mental health issues like stress, anxiety and depression, and academic struggles, ultimately affecting cognitive and emotional development. Adults can navigate challenging environments using their coping skills.

SUGGESTIONS:

The government should provide adequate security and improve the schools in poor neighbourhoods.

It is essential for parents to provide a secure and nurturing environment for their children to thrive.

Adults require a safe environment to mitigate unnecessary stress that will impact their lives negatively.

CHILD MARRIAGE

In numerous countries and communities, girl children are forced into early marriages due to numerous factors such as poverty and debt repayment. Cultural and religious beliefs also contribute to forced marriages in some communities.

Girl children often lack a voice in marriage arrangements, facing consequences for refusal. It is either they face an ultimatum: accept forced marriage or face consequences at home. Consequently, in some cases, a number of them run away from home.

Child marriage has devastating consequences for young girls. One of its most serious effects is child rape, as minors cannot provide informed sexual consent. Girls who give birth at a young age face serious health challenges. Their bodies are not developed enough, resulting in health issues, such as vesico-vagina fistula, a condition causing involuntary urine leakage through the vagina.

Young girls forced into marriage face abuse and exploitation by their older husbands, being coerced into uncomfortable and harmful situations. They are at risk of contracting sexually transmitted diseases.

Child brides often face isolation, battling loneliness due to their circumstances. Many are at risk of developing severe psychological disorders. Some often struggle with low self-esteem and face an increased risk of substance abuse due to their hostile environment.

SUGGESTIONS:

There is a need for the government to prohibit and enforce laws protecting girl children and ending child marriage.

There is a pressing need to raise awareness in communities and religious groups that condone child marriage, emphasising its harmful effects. However, the ultimate responsibility lies with governments to enact and enforce laws prohibiting child marriage.

It is of utmost priority that the government provides comprehensive welfare programs, ensuring young girls from disadvantaged backgrounds receive education and care until they reach the legal age of marriage.

HOMELESSNESS

Unfavourable circumstances force people to live in precarious outdoor conditions, deprived of a safe and comfortable living environment. Living conditions may include streets, parks, temporary shelters, or camps. Such environments are neither secure nor suitable for living, particularly for families with children.

Some of the circumstances that can lead to homelessness include:

Lack of Jobs.

Poverty.

Natural disasters (where people will take shelter in a camp).

Temporary living conditions lack essential security and

privacy, falling short of the comfort and stability provided by a permanent home. People are exposed to risks depending on the environment in which they take shelter.

Children may be vulnerable to various forms of abuse and can adopt unhealthy behaviours by observing their surroundings. Prolonged exposure to such environments can significantly affect children's development. They face the potential risk of mental health issues including anxiety, depression, and loneliness.

Adults are also exposed to social risks such as:
1. Violence.
2. Loneliness.
3. Stigma.
4. Discrimination.
5. Mental health challenges.

SUGGESTIONS:

It is expedient that the government makes available conducive and adequate temporary accommodation for homeless individuals and families. This should include disaster-affected individuals in camps while ensuring a safe and convenient space for people to live in. People must ensure that they are not isolated from family, friends, and others. In some cases, and circumstances, a family/friends network can provide temporary accommodation for someone as this can also foster a support system to protect their emotional needs.

PREGNANCY/IVF/POST-PARTUM DEPRESSION

Pregnancy presents various challenges. While some women may experience a relatively smooth journey, others face numerous difficulties before, during, and after pregnancy that can negatively impact their mental well-being. Some women struggle with natural conception due to factors like age, health issues, or other circumstances.

Some single women may choose to take proactive steps if they're approaching menopause and haven't married or had children.

At this stage, natural conception becomes challenging, making Assisted Reproduction (IVF) a viable option, thanks to advancements in medical technology. This procedure is costly and complex with no guarantee of a 100% success rate. When a couple decides to use IVF, the woman will undergo several preparatory steps and hormonal injections. The fertility process may involve retrieving her own eggs or using donor eggs. Either option can impose significant physical and emotional demands on the woman.

If the procedure is successful, the joy of childbirth will overshadow all the pressures endured. But if it fails, there is a feeling of grief and sadness. It is a stressful moment for the woman and her partner. Some women succeed on their first try, while others achieve success on their second, third, fourth or fifth attempts, depending on their ability to cover the costs. In some cases, this option may not be viable for the woman. Surrogacy then becomes a consideration. In this case, another woman will carry the pregnancy to term based on arrangements made between the couple involved and the surrogate.

Several factors are considered in the choice of what fertility treatment to opt for. Choosing whether to use donated eggs and sperm is one of the decisions that need to be taken. Infertility struggles are far from easy. Often, they lead to feelings of isolation, anxiety and depression. When procedures fail, couples experience crushing disappointment, oscillating between hope and despair.

Postpartum depression affects many women after childbirth, yet some people remain unaware of this condition. Often, society expects new mothers to feel happy and excited after giving birth, but in reality, many struggle with unexpected emotional challenges.

Some of the challenges they experience include:

Trouble sleeping.

Sleepless nights

They have a challenge forming an emotional connection with the baby.

They experience anxiety and mood swings which can also lead to depression.

They may experience overeating or a decreased appetite.

Women at risk of postpartum depression may have certain factors that increase their vulnerability:

1. Previous history of depression or emotional issues.

2. Genetic predisposition.

3. Multiple births (e.g. twins or triplets).

4. Hormonal fluctuations and changes.

SUGGESTIONS:

Friends and family should offer emotional support to women going through pregnancy or IVF challenges.

It is essential to foster strength, not isolation.

For a thriving relationship, couples should strive for active support and genuine communication.

It is essential to seek professional help from a therapist or specialised professionals experienced in supporting women's issues.

Additionally, joining a support group can be highly beneficial for them.

Setting healthy boundaries is crucial. Family and friends should refrain from asking married couples about their decision to have children or why they have not had any children.

IN-LAW RELATIONSHIPS

Mothers often serve as primary caregivers. Some find it challenging to let go of this role, extending their caregiving to their sons' families after marriage. This often creates conflict because the wife prefers decision-making authority, rather than the husband taking advice from his mother. This situation often creates tension between the wife and mother-in-law. In some cases, the wife may feel jealous if the husband is particularly close to his mother, leading her to try various means to break the bond. Some women are raised in unhealthy environments marked by destructive competition, conflict, and harmful parenting practices. As a result, their understanding of love becomes skewed, prioritizing exclusive affection for themselves above all others.

So, the mother-son bond is always a threat. Some even wish their potential mother-in-law dead. They will prefer a partner whose mother has passed away or someone who is not particularly close to their mother. Also, they tend to extend the attitude to the man's family and friends and may resort to manipulation, including lying, to drive a wedge between their partner and their loved ones. This is all to make their partners focus on their children and family and select close friends.

This is mostly a subtle war many women engage in. After marriage, they may collect personal details about their spouses' family and friends, which they may subsequently exploit to manipulate their husbands.

Some men can be naïve during the early stages of a relationship and may share excessive information about their siblings, parents, friends, colleagues, and others with their spouse during the honeymoon phase - including details that are meant to remain private between them and their siblings or friends.

Once the man finds himself trapped, it is challenging to escape. Typically, he succumbs to his wife's demands, becomes loyal, and then starts creating distance between himself and his siblings. He may pick unnecessary fights to justify his struggles connecting with his siblings.

Some individuals may resist the manipulative system and choose to maintain relationships with their family and friends, while also allowing their partner to do the same. The friction will persist as some manipulative wives may continue to impose their will, causing ongoing conflict and discomfort at home. For some women, their siblings and parents are welcome in their homes anytime, freely interacting with their children. In contrast, their husband's family 'needs to apply for a visa and get it approved' specifying arrival and departure times to gain approval.

Typically, a man's parents, particularly his mother, have concerns about their incoming daughter-in-law, based on past experiences. They know some daughters-in-law who fuel sibling rivalry when their husbands appear more successful than others. Their plan is to control finances, benefiting only themselves, their family and siblings, while disregarding others whose sacrifices contributed to their husband's success.

Many mothers experience distress when they notice their sons behaving differently towards them or their siblings after marriage. Ironically, when financial struggles arise, the same woman will advocate for closer ties with her husband's family because of her self-interest.

Some parents deeply rooted in culture and tradition prefer a daughter-in-law who shares and respects their values, rather than one who is indifferent.

It is a life-long circle. Today's daughter-in-law becomes

tomorrow's mother-in-law, walking in similar shoes. Her perspective will shift when she considers her future daughter-in-law. She ponders thus, "Is she going to be a builder or a destroyer of the family?"

The negative impact of relationships with in-laws generates stress, anxiety, and conflicts.

SUGGESTIONS:

Establishing healthy boundaries and mutual empathy is essential on both sides.

A united front is crucial for couples to treat both sets of in-laws equally.

Seek therapy when needed.

Have a sound conflict resolution system.

MARRIAGE/RELATIONSHIP

Marriage demands total attention to foster a stable, happy, and prosperous relationship. The way we take time to practice healthy living is also applicable to marriage - no half-measures!

Both parties involved need to be dedicated to making it work. It is not left for one to devote time and effort, and the other to behave selfishly without considering its impact on the union. When two people are united in a relationship, conflict is bound to occur due to differing cultural backgrounds. They will have unique experiences, independent habits, and distinct worldviews.

If conflict is not properly managed, it negatively impacts the relationship, and it can lead to many consequences, like feelings of rejection. Furthermore, it increases the stress hormones and leads to unrest and depression. Consequently, it affects the emotional bond between the partners. Unaddressed childhood traumas originating from unguarded parenting can lead adults to bring unhealthy patterns into their relationships. Unresolved trauma can lead individuals to unleash anger, stress, and frustration on their partners.

Someone with self-centred tendencies and narcissistic traits often exhibits controlling behaviours, including:

Key Traits

1. **Condescending attitude:** Looking down on others.
2. **Grandiosity:** Believing they are unique or superior.
3. **Emotional manipulation:** Using silent treatment.
4. **Lack of gratitude:** Never appreciating efforts or kindness shown to them.

Their actions erode others' self-esteem and confidence, triggering mental health concerns.

Challenges that will be encountered in relationships are numerous:

Relationships with siblings and relatives, and how they are handled will depend on the stress they can cause in marriage.

Conflicts may arise from contrasting parenting styles, particularly when one partner enforces discipline and the other is more indulgent.

Financial management is crucial. Reversal of traditional roles (whereby the woman begins to earn more than the man who is regarded as the breadwinner) can stress marriages if not handled carefully. There will be pressure on the man to earn more than the wife, whether it is within his power to do so or not.

Also, many men struggle with feelings of inadequacy when their wife is the breadwinner or earns far more than them.

SUGGESTIONS:
Parents need to have a united front in the training of

children.

Marriage is a collective project, and everyone needs to work equally.

Couples should seek counselling when it is required.

Establish loving boundaries and respect each other's family and friend networks.

Practise Self-care.

PATERNITY FRAUD

This refers to a situation where a mother deceives a man into accepting a child as his own, driven by ulterior motives. Some women intentionally 'pin' the paternity of the child on a successful man for personal benefits. These benefits include child support and other advantages associated with having a child with a successful individual.

Out of ignorance, some women commit fraud as they assume the person is the biological father.

The negative impact is devastating for a man who has formed a bond with the child and invested so much, only to find out one day, that he is not the biological father. It is heart-wrenching!

Some women, fearful of uncertainty surrounding their child's paternity, may attribute it to a previous sexual partner, often the one (owing to the need of a child) most willing or able to assume parental responsibilities, without questioning or verifying paternity.

The emotional stress the victim undergoes is often quite strenuous, coupled with the social stigma that tags along with such cases. Also, if the child is an adult, the information tends to affect their emotional state and can lead to depression or self-harm.

SUGGESTIONS:

There is a need for strong laws to ensure penalties for

women who engage in paternity fraud.

Depending on the societal context or jurisdiction, DNA testing may be recommended or required at birth to confirm paternity.

Support for victims of paternity fraud, including the wrongly accused man and the child, is crucial.

MIDLIFE CRISIS

A midlife crisis is a time of inner turmoil or self-reflection about our life choices and identity. The experience can be stressful and daunting, and it is also a time of self-reflection and growth. Women and men both experience a midlife crisis. It can be mild or severe, with significant life changes and consequences that may occur around 40 and 60.

Some of the noticeable signs include:

Regret over past decisions or actions.

Impulsive actions: Making sudden, uninformed decisions, such as buying luxury items (cars, houses) or taking drastic measures without careful consideration.

Some individuals may experience apathy and a loss of interest in life.

Some will reminisce on things they have done in the past.

Some individuals crave excitement and adventure, potentially leading them to engage in extramarital affairs.

Some individuals may make spontaneous decisions, such as ending their marriage or resigning from their job to pursue an alternative path.

There may be an increase or decrease in sex drive.

Some individuals become fixated on their appearance, striving to look younger through their dress and overall aesthetics.

Feelings of anxiety, stress, and sadness are common.

Women experience menopause during that period, and

a lot of hormonal changes may occur that will affect their mood.

Some may stop caring about their looks and dressing.

Also, there may be weight changes.

SUGGESTIONS:

Reframe their view and perception of mid-life crisis and how they see the process of ageing.

Acceptance of things beyond their control.

Have a plan, and stick to it with a sense of purpose.

Take care of their overall health.

Understand that they need not act on any thought in their head.

Practise mindfulness, meditation, and self-control.

Settle for Treatment options for women during menopause.

Seek therapy when needed.

DIVORCE/SEPARATION

Divorce is a stressful and challenging time in a couple's life, and it has a long-lasting effect on their mental health. It also has an adverse impact on the lives of the children. Divorce can cause a lot of havoc on mental health, like anxiety, depression, anger, guilt, and low self-esteem.

It will affect children's academic performance as they tend to have low self-esteem.

Feelings of anxiety and a tendency to withdraw from others may occur.

They exhibit aggressive behaviour.

SUGGESTIONS:

Never isolate oneself after a divorce.

Be in touch with family and friends and address their emotional, spiritual, and physical needs.

Seek counselling, if needed.

Maintain healthy boundaries.

Parents need to create a safe environment for their children.

Maintain a stable routine for the children and protect them from toxic encounters with ex-partners.

BULLYING / CYBERBULLYING

Bullying involves intentional, repeated, and unwarranted attacks targeting vulnerable individuals. It includes physical and verbal abuse, name-calling, and threats. Cyberbullying involves the use of email, social media, and chat rooms to perpetuate bullying. Bullying can take place in the workplace, not only in the school environment. Bullying includes aggressive behaviours like:

1. Undermining others' works.
2. Abusing authority.
3. Verbal abuse.

Bullying involves both physical attacks and verbal abuse. Bullying can take many forms, including exclusion from a peer group or blackmail.

It creates a cycle whereby someone bullied earlier will turn around to bully others when the opportunity comes.

Bullies lack empathy, and they tend to target vulnerable individuals like people with disabilities, LGBTQ+, and immigrants.

Parents need to watch out for signs indicating that their children are being bullied. Bullying has devastating effects on victims, manifesting physically as stomachaches, headaches, and general body pains.

Psychological signs include anxiety, sadness, trouble sleeping, feelings of helplessness, and loneliness. Also, their schoolwork will be affected by poor academic performance.

Bullying can lead to suicidal thoughts or suicide.

SUGGESTIONS:

The victims must be assured that they will not be blamed for being bullied.

Parents must notify school authorities immediately and ensure serious action is taken.

Effective therapeutic interventions are crucial to support victims in overcoming challenges and developing essential coping skills for long-term resilience.

The bullies in question require psychological evaluation and support to manage aggression and develop healthier coping mechanisms.

They need help to address other unhealthy coping skills that they have acquired.

Also, we must collectively reject bullying in all its forms, whether in school or the workplace.

SPIRITUAL ABUSE

Any abuse within the religious environment is classified as spiritual abuse. It can occur in many ways. It can be the manipulation of member to part with their money or demanding absolute loyalty without objection.

Religious leaders use Bible quotations to keep their members in check. They reference that anointing flows from top to bottom, and to be blessed and succeed, you must honour your spiritual leaders. This tends to create a power dynamic that they abuse. So, on the one hand, they are the anointed of God, the superior ones, and the people will depend on them if they want to succeed. Thus, their word is law, and the members always look up to them for spiritual protection, prayers, and blessings. They exploit members' dependence on them to enrich themselves and satisfy their desires.

Brainwashed members comply with orders, even when unjust, often driven by fear. So, in a situation where the religious leader demands money or sexual favours from women or young teenagers, they find it hard to resist.

Members often disregard their own judgement and conscience, complying with the religious leader's directives. This is because their minds are already controlled by the leader's mind in that aspect. They have lost their willpower and replaced it with the spiritual leader's will. What the spiritual leaders say, matters more than anything else.

Alternatively, religious leaders position themselves as spiritual guardians or parents to their members. Consequently, members view their spiritual leaders with absolute respect and submission, akin to their biological parents. Thus, leaving the congregation becomes tough for the members as it appears like they are leaving their parents and family.

Also, the fear of ostracising anyone with a contrary view puts them in check. Some religious leaders will encourage their members to excommunicate anyone who disobeys their order or leaves their fold. Therefore, leaving behind long-standing family and friend connections makes it difficult for some individuals to exit unhealthy congregations.

Many religious leaders equate the concept of 'leaders' fruitfulness in the Bible' to material possessions and money. They admonish the congregation that wealth is a sign of God's blessing. This tends to put a lot of pressure on members to be in their leader's excellent book, by showcasing their latest cars and houses and giving huge tithes and offerings to the church.

Some individuals engage in fraudulent acts to acquire these possessions so long as they are touted as examples of God's blessing in the church. They will relate with the religious leaders, and others would like to 'make it' to belong to the same level and have access to their leaders. This manifests in many churches, and the leaders brag that the measure of fruitfulness is evident in their midst. With expensive church buildings, fleets of luxury cars, private jets, and the number of members, it becomes a 'bragging right' that God answers their prayers.

Amid so much hype by religious leaders, those who are abused find it difficult to speak up, as no one will listen to them, or they will be accused of trying to pull a man of God down. They become depressed, angry, and isolated. Some will develop panic attacks while some will leave the congregation and face the consequences rather than witnessing a fake environment that is stressful and damaging to their mental health.

SUGGESTIONS:
Therapy can aid survivors of prolonged abuse within environments where they once placed their trust and faith.

Reaching out to others is very important.

People should avoid being isolated by any religious leader or congregation as this can be a means to control and manipulate members.

People should ensure that no religious leader controls them. They should remember that they have free will, as given by God. Also, everyone should know that all men are equal in God's eyes.

HIGH FUNCTIONING ANXIETY

This refers to people who function well in their daily lives but experience anxiety. It motivates the person to work hard to succeed in life rather than being crippled with fear. It has a positive and negative side.

Some of the positives include:

1. Organisational skills.
2. Passionate nature.
3. Punctuality.
4. Outgoing personality.
5. High achievement orientation.
6. Empathy.
Some of the negatives include:
1. Overthinking.
2. Difficulty relaxing.
3. Sleep problems.
4. Undue comparison with others.
5. Difficulty refusing requests.
6. Procrastination.
7. The risk of alcohol or drug abuse.
Some of the causes include:
The feeling of loss like death.
Relationship problems.
Stress.
History of anxiety.
High parental expectations are one of the causes of high-functioning anxiety in teens.

SUGGESTIONS:

The use of stress management techniques such as:
Mindfulness meditation.
Thoughts reframing.
Therapy and a strong support system.
A healthy lifestyle includes eating well, sleeping well, and exercising
Teens need adult guidance in coming to terms with any stresses in their lives. Learning good coping skills is crucial.

LGBTQ+

Gender non-conforming and LGBTQ+ people are

at risk of having mental health problems. This is due to the stresses they undergo in society based on their choices and chosen way of life. The transition will affect the entire family dynamics. Many conflicts in the family will arise based on the family values and belief system. Many will not tolerate or support such a move, and in some communities and cultures, it is regarded as an abomination. In some religious communities, it is considered a sin. This fosters an environment where individuals conceal their true identity to evade potential consequences.

Adults have the freedom to make their own choices and adopt any lifestyle they prefer. Transition as a child or young teen poses significant challenges for families. Many parents know that the age of consent for sexual activity is 16 or 18 in most civilised countries. This creates significant challenges for them when young teens are encouraged to start the transition as early as 12 or 13, These are still children, so allowing children to make permanent decisions at such a young age, based solely on their emotions, may have a long-lasting impact on their lives. There are instances of some who regretted undergoing treatments when they were so young. They accuse authorities of permitting irreversible choices without adequate guidance, leading to regret and dissatisfaction in adulthood. The encouragement of puberty blockers as early as 12yrs and 13yrs is what many people and families are concerned about.

Some of the challenges they face which will have an impact on their life include:

They are at greater risk of experiencing hate crimes as they are targeted owing to their chosen identities.

They will face isolation and loneliness in many families and communities that frown at such lifestyle choices.

The stress of coming out initially will make them anxious

for a long while.

They will face discrimination from people, and it may affect them in some workplaces and events.

Due to some of these challenges they may encounter, the stress of all those experiences will put them at risk of several mental health challenges.

Anxiety and depression will affect both the young and old with a resultant effect on their quality of life.

Academic performance will suffer.

There will be feelings of loneliness and hopelessness.

Bullying and lack of support can cause traumatic experiences for them.

They are at high risk of eating disorders and attempted suicide.

Others may struggle with drug and alcohol addiction, using substances as an unhealthy coping strategy to manage stress, emotions or trauma.

SUGGESTIONS:

Adults deserve government protection and support for their lifestyle choices, as everyone has the right to their choices, so long they do not infringe on others.

It is important for the government to investigate gender reassignment surgery on young teens who are not up to the age of sexual consent. These life-altering decisions need to be made as an adult in the same way the age of consent is approved. This is based on the understanding that the person can make decisions with the knowledge of the risk involved.

People need to be empathetic towards others who do not have the same identity and choices in lifestyle.

Everyone should decide the direction of their life based on their faith, values, and beliefs.

We need to stop judging others and focus on our own lives.

Children need to be protected amid so many changes in the world. They should be protected as much as possible from experiencing some lifestyle choices or ways of life. This is to ensure they are of age to make decisions on the direction of their own life.

NEURODEVELOPMENTAL DISABILITY

Children with neurodevelopmental disabilities face a lot of challenges. The same applies to their families. The disorder affects how the brain functions, impacting cognitive, social, and emotional behaviour. Examples are autism, attention deficit/hyperactivity disorder, and many others, including cerebral palsy and learning disorder.

The disorders can persist into adulthood. Some of the features include behaviour issues, learning and speech challenges, and poor social skills. They may also have self-esteem issues, poor sleep, sometimes refusal of food, isolation, and poor academic performance.

Parents also experience stressful moments trying to figure out the challenges, how to handle them, and the financial cost.

SUGGESTIONS:

Early diagnosis is very crucial in management, and to reduce stress on both individuals with ND and their parents.

Parents need to support each other and the child. The stress of managing the situation can affect the marriage if they are not mindful.

Treatment options include exercise, good food, medications, and the adoption of healthy habits for the child.

Therapy is needed for both the teens and adults affected.

PHYSICAL DISABILITY

Disabled people are among the vulnerable groups at risk

of having mental health issues. There are a lot of challenges faced by disabled people which affect them adversely. Some places are not accessible to them; wheelchair users cannot enter a building without a lift as they cannot use the stairs, thereby restricting access to the place.

Some barriers or steps will be difficult for a blind person to navigate without someone assisting them. Some are limited in terms of schools to attend and course of study. Their job opportunities are limited due to their disability. They face a lot of discrimination and stigma in many places. This affects their social interactions, resulting in loneliness and isolation.

Due to the many challenges they encounter, they experience stress and anxiety, and some have problems with their relationships. They may be depressed and experience trauma.

SUGGESTIONS:

There is a growing need for targeted mental health awareness initiatives catering to individuals with disabilities, empowering them with coping strategies and acceptance.

The government needs to pass strong laws protecting the interests of the disabled. It must address their access to many places and discrimination in workplaces and other areas.

People must be empathetic and support people with disabilities in their environment or anywhere they encounter them.

People should stop prejudice and stereotypes directed at people with disabilities.

Persons with disability need a robust support system to help them. They must be aware of new opportunities and any development that can improve their well-being.

ALBINISM

Albinism is a rare genetic disorder resulting from low

melanin pigments. People with albinism have pale skin, hair, eyes, light sensitivity, crossed eyes, and vision problems. Some of the challenges they face include vision problems, skin problems, and social stigma. This puts them at risk of isolation, anxiety, depression, and other mental health issues.

In some African communities, they are targeted, killed, and used for ritual purposes. So, in those environments, they live in a state of fear/panic, worsening their mental health.

SUGGESTIONS:

There is a need for support from family, friends, and community for people with Albinism. The government needs to protect and safeguard the lives of Albino in countries where they are at risk of being used for ritual purposes.

Albinos must wear hats, use umbrellas when necessary, and stay out of the sun as much as possible.

They need to go for counselling if they are in distress.

They need to practice self-care: and taking care of their spiritual, mental, and physical well-being.

RACISM /DISCRIMINATION

The long-term stressful effect of racism and discrimination on an individual can lead to serious mental health challenges.

Racism can occur in many ways:

It can be through institutions or government policies that affect a particular race; or the justice system, the media, and the financial system, which makes things more challenging for the group.

Law enforcement agents may profile people of particular races.

Getting credit is challenging and at high interest if approved.

They experience stigma, as their neighbourhood is usually avoided and viewed as a dangerous place. Some are scared to interact with them and avoid close contact. In some cases, some oppressed people internalise racism and even believe they have a problem. This will lead to low self-esteem and negative self-talk.

Institutional racism is always present, creating a state whereby the individual is perpetually under stress. These stresses will cause the person to be depressed, anxious, and on edge for further discriminatory action.

There is a feeling of anger against the unjust system.

There's the likelihood of alcohol and drug abuse to numb the feelings.

It creates a state of hopelessness about the future.

SUGGESTIONS:

There is a need for laws to enforce a total ban on all forms of discrimination against anybody based on race, gender, etc.

There is a need for many social organisations/institutions to champion and protect the interests of the oppressed.

It is crucial for oppressors to acknowledge and understand the devastating impact of their actions on marginalised groups, and to engage in empathy by putting themselves in others' shoes.

The oppressed need adequate support.

They need to learn vital coping skills to avoid the devastating impact of racism on their mental health.

WAR

The impact of war and associated violence on the mental health of the civilian population is very devastating. It affects everyone, including the soldiers involved, the medical staff, and even the humanitarian agencies working in the battlefield.

Vulnerable groups like children, women, and people with disabilities are more affected than men. Children rely on their parents for support, and during the war, the death of the parents will expose the children to severe traumatic experiences resulting in anxiety, and depression. They constantly live in a state of fear and terror, not knowing what will happen next. This may lead to a lot of mental health issues. The loss of body parts during the war will put the individual in a traumatic state. War destroys the lives of people and retards development. Lack of adequate sleep and nutrition seriously impacts the lives of people, putting them at risk of physical and mental health problems.

The traumatic experience tends to last even after the war is over and can affect their lives years after the conflict.

SUGGESTIONS:

There is a need for all sides in a war to consider other options, putting into consideration the dangers of war on the lives of the people.

There is a need for humanitarian agencies to offer counselling and therapy solutions, not only the provision of food and medical supplies.

There should be provision of an adequate support system for victims of war, during and after the conflict. Enhancing community networks provides vital support and assistance to individuals impacted by conflict.

SOCIAL MEDIA / TECHNOLOGY

Technology is excellent and enhances productivity and quality of life, but negative uses can harm mental health. Social media helps people communicate, advertise, and show their talent. It also allows people to be accepted by joining support groups, or online associations. Wrong use can be dangerous as it can lead to bullying (cyberbullying) and other harmful purposes, including exploitation of teenagers, grooming, fraud, scams, etc.

Moderation is vital, but excessive use of social media comes with a lot of consequences, as it can lead to loneliness, anxiety, and the risk of going into depression.

Also, it leads to feelings of inadequacy when you start comparing yourself to others. Constantly being online to stay updated can lead to addiction, negatively impacting work productivity, sleep, and real-time relationships.

It encourages self-centeredness, as people will always focus on improving their image and lives to appear remarkable in their selfies.

Some use it as a coping skill to avoid connection with people.

Some people engage in dangerous behaviour to gain followers, likes, and shares. They post fake news and pictures of people in embarrassing positions and take photos and videos of accident victims to post online rather than offering a helping hand.

Excessive social media and technology use can trigger the brain's reward centres, releasing feel-good chemicals that may contribute to addiction.

SUGGESTIONS:

The most significant risk of social media and technology is that talented engineers and behavioural scientists design them to be addictive.

As you scroll or click, the algorithm will produce more of the information you want, and you will be immersed beyond the time you allocated for it. Also, notifications and push messages will always attract your attention, making you develop a short attention span.

The government needs to enact strong laws to checkmate some of the excesses of these platforms.

An acceptable age for children to access social media is likely in their late teens.

People should ask themselves serious questions about the necessity of every post.

Teenagers should be allotted time to use social media. Parents can try to talk to them about this so they will not depend on it. Teenagers should also spend time with people in real-time.

SCHOOL AND MASS SHOOTING

School and mass shooting causes are very complex, and it is not about gun control and mental health issues alone.

Some of the circumstances that may lead people to engage in shootings include:

Poor family values, characterised by dysfunctional dynamics and toxic environments, make it challenging to raise children.

In some families, there is a lack of a father figure to guide and mentor the male child.

Some children require training in effective coping skills to better navigate life's challenges.

Bullying plays a role, as well, as it affects the mental health of the victim, leaving the individual stressed out, anxious, fearful, and isolated. There will be a sense of anger towards the bullies, and the system they assume did not protect them. This will lead some to commit such atrocities against society.

Additionally, some individuals have suffered domestic abuse and witnessed violence either at home or in their community.

There are many instances of radicalisation where individuals learn to commit terrible acts from the internet.

SUGGESTIONS:

There is a need to restrict gun access to dangerous or mentally challenged individuals. Also, the same applies to people with a history of violence.

Equipping young people with coping skills early is necessary so they will not be pushed to the brink by any challenge they may encounter.

We must educate students about the dangers of bullying, emphasizing its risks to victims, perpetrators, and bystanders. This is because someone who is bullied and filled with rage may engage in mass shootings as a form of vendetta.

There is a need for counselling services for at-risk students and therapy for individuals.

Additionally, a robust support system is necessary in today's increasingly individualistic world.

TRAUMA

Trauma is defined as any fearful, stressful event that can put one at risk and is dangerous, and life-threatening. It causes a lot of emotional and physical symptoms. Not everyone develops trauma after an event. It depends on a whole lot of circumstances. Some traumas can be a single terrifying event, or it can be an ongoing affair like domestic violence, bullying, etc., or may result from a whole lot of other incidents.

Some emotional responses to trauma are hopelessness, numbness, difficulty concentrating, fear, sadness, anger, and denial. Accompanying physical signs are sweating, racing heartbeat, digestive issues, headaches, shakiness, racing thoughts, and shallow breathing.

Some of the causes of trauma are sexual abuse, physical bullying, loss of a loved one, accidents, violent attacks, natural disasters, and harassment. When the symptoms persist after the stressful event, it results in post-traumatic stress disorder. This results in flashbacks and relieving the painful event.

SUGGESTIONS:

Therapy is recommended, such as helping people change their negative thoughts to positive thoughts to influence their behaviour positively.

Use of medication.

Adoption of a healthy lifestyle.

Practising mindfulness exercises and learning good coping skills.

MULTITASKING

It is stressful trying to do two or more things at the same time. Our brains function well when we focus on one task alone. Multitasking consumes brain energy and makes us more likely to be distracted frequently. It is tasking on the brain and affects our attention span, leading to poor concentration. It also makes us prone to anxiety and can lead to a state of chronic stress if it becomes the norm. There will be a loss of focus, poor decisions, low quality of work.

SUGGESTIONS:

Avoid distractions in all its forms.

Focus on one thing at a time.

Put away anything that distracts you while working or reading, like gadgets.

Practise mindfulness meditation.

VALIDATION/SHOW-OFF

People seek validation to boost their self-esteem, share accomplishments, or cover their insecurities. The quest for validation can push people toward unhealthy habits like faking their lifestyle and portraying who they are not. Some attach their self-worth to appraisals from people. There's always constant pressure to get people's attention, which can be quite stressful. If they receive positive compliments, they feel good about themselves. If it is negative comments, it tends to affect their self-esteem, which can lead to depression.

Some of the reasons for external validation:

The need to be recognised and appreciated.

Sense of inferiority, low self-esteem, and lack of confidence push people to seek external validation.

Insecurity drives individuals to showcase their achievements and success, seeking commendation to temporarily boost their self-worth.

However, since the underlying issues remain unaddressed, this cycle of seeking validation repeats itself.

SUGGESTIONS::

People need self-confidence and should base their self-esteem on their beliefs and inner character.

Avoid the need for comparison.

Stop undue competition in areas such as wealth, power, looks, etc.

Try to focus on their goals, and focus less on what others are doing.

GOVERNANCE

Good governance will result in good development, solid and responsive institutions, and a good justice and welfare system. It involves all the good attributes of a just society.

Bad governance, on the other hand, will create an oppressive atmosphere that will affect the citizens. There will be weak institutions, corruption, inequalities, poverty, and other weaknesses in governance. There is a lack of transparency and trust in the government.

The presence of bad leadership coupled with corruption will result in inadequate infrastructure for the people. Hence, access to quality care will be stressful for citizens. Also, the high poverty rate will put tremendous stress on people to get the basic things of life. Vulnerable people will pass through stress to eat, have a quality education, get suitable housing, and secure good jobs to pay their bills. This tends to affect their mental state, seriously. The sense of being powerless to do anything, trapped in poverty, struggle to survive is always devastating to their health. It can lead to social unrest, demonstrations, or strike actions by workers' unions.

SUGGESTIONS:

Need for accountability in governance.

The institutions need to be strengthened.

Active participation in the political process is crucial for electing credible leaders.

Some constitutional reforms may be needed in some cases.

CANCEL CULTURE

Cancel culture involves removing support for individuals, organisations, and companies based on their actions or positions deemed offensive to those cancelling them. It is a form of boycott. It can take different forms such as boycotting products, pressuring companies to stop sponsoring someone, cancelling their endorsement, or public appearance of the persons targeted.

Some of the positive effects are:

They are avenues for oppressed people to seek justice, such as teaching oppressors a lesson by publicly exposing them.

It is a teaching moment for the oppressors to learn and amend their ways.

It gives voice to the oppressed to make their positions known to all and rally widespread support.

This approach sparks positive change by shedding light on a specific issue, exposing its harmful effects, and rallying public awareness.

Some of the negative sides are:

False cancellation can have devastating consequences, causing innocent individuals significant emotional distress, anxiety, and depression.

Cancel Culture is a harmful form of bullying that can escalate into hate speech and targeted attacks, causing significant emotional distress and potentially leading to psychological harm, stress and vulnerability.

In some cases, cancel culture targets people who disagree with those who want them cancelled.

SUGGESTIONS:

There is a need to allow a contrary view instead of punishing someone for having a different view.

Let the focus be on ideas or issues at stake, not attacks on individuals or companies.

We need to respect each other irrespective of the group we belong.

ADDICTION

Addiction is a condition that involves a constant quest for an activity or taking something despite it being harmful. It is a severe condition that will impact a person's health.

Some of the things that people are likely to be addicted to are things like drugs and alcohol, activities like sex, shopping, use of the internet, eating, pornography, and wild lifestyles.

Some signs to watch out for are difficulty stopping an activity, being preoccupied with an activity, intense craving for a drug or substance, isolation, and behavioural patterns.

The way our brain's reward centre works helps in the development of addiction to a substance or activity if not properly guided. Good and sweet things trigger the feel-good hormone, making us feel good. Stuff, like some drugs, cause an increase in the feel-good hormone, thereby making us take it and feel good. The same thing applies to food, sex, and other activities. That is why some may be addicted to sex and find it difficult to control themselves. Also, some mental health conditions and genetic and environmental influences help the development of addictions.

SUGGESTIONS:

Raising awareness that everything sweet has its negative implications too.

There is a need for moderation in everything, whether food, sex, exercise, etc.

Treatment using medications, or therapy for the addicted.

Support groups to help people with addictive behaviour.

Self-care and developing solid coping skills to avoid being addicted to anything.

Be supportive of persons passing through the challenge.

LONELINESS

Loneliness is not about being alone; it can be felt among people or family. It can last a limited time or be chronic and last a long time. It is an intense feeling.

Loneliness can result from the following:

The loss of a loved one.

The reliance on social media instead of real connection.

Inability to make friends.

The mindset.

It can happen owing to a change of location, a new place, school, etc.

Some of the adverse effects are:

Increase in stress level and risk of depression.

Drug and alcohol abuse.

Antisocial behaviour.

Increased risk of suicidal thoughts.

SUGGESTIONS:
Maintain good relationships with family and friends.
Engage in community activities.
Volunteer for some organisations.
Treatments include therapy to learn how to cope with the situation and overcome the fear of socialising.

INFLUENCER CULTURE

People with large social media followers use their large following to influence their followers' choices, opinions, and lifestyles. They can be known celebrities, stars, or everyday people with large followers on any social media platform.

Influencers can motivate others to aspire to create businesses or their content online. Followers can learn a lot of information on complex subject matters from the influencers they follow. The things they promote can improve their followers' creativity and create an avenue for communication from many people.

Influencers' promotion of substandard goods and services is one of the dangers of influencer marketing. Many are interested in the money they will make, not the quality or authenticity of the product they endorse. It helps promote consumerism and a show-off lifestyle. Many would like to live like the influencers they follow and try to make money and buy possessions for unnecessary show-offs. The images projected by influencers are well-packaged and edited. Many followers will find it challenging to meet the standards the influencer projects on social media. This will put unnecessary stress and pressure on them to meet a complex and unreal standard. This might lead to a state of anxiety and chronic stress.

SUGGESTIONS:
Social Media influencers need to present an authentic

image.

Be accurate in their interaction and avoid promoting harmful content for monetary benefit.

People need to know that influencers are all about business and may even promote a product they do not use because of monetary gain.

People should try to live a lifestyle they can afford without looking at anybody for inspiration.

People should maintain genuine relationships offline, and reduce the time spent on social media.

BURN OUT

When you feel tired, stressed, and exhausted, it can be challenging to complete a task. The prolonged stress associated with burnout affects our overall health.

Some symptoms are feeling exhausted, which can affect one's work and home life. Feelings of helplessness and demotivation emerge, causing a loss of interest in previously enjoyed activities.

There is a tendency to withdraw from responsibilities. There is an urge to procrastinate and delay one's activities. There are some physical signs like headaches, disturbances in sleep, etc. There's a sense of frustration and anger.

Some of the risk factors are:

Perfectionism and having a very high standard, pose challenges to meet.

Negative views and beliefs about life.

Lack of support or recognition of effort at work or home.

Not living a balanced life, no time for work, leisure, and other activities.

Working in a high-pressure field or job that is demanding.

SUGGESTIONS:

Create strict boundaries between work, home, leisure,

and other activities.

Always connect with people, friends, families, etc.

Support and be part of a charitable course.

Be on good terms with colleagues at work.

Practise healthy living.

BODY SHAMING

This involves making negative comments about someone's appearance, or body shape, whether by jokes, teasing, or mockery. Body shaming can be face-to-face or via social media. It can be from strangers, friends, siblings or parents.

Some of the causes are high parental expectations which can sometimes translate into unhealthy pressure on children. Examples of body shaming include mocking a child's weight or appearance, such as calling them 'fat' or criticising their personal grooming. Siblings may also perpetuate body shaming by making derogatory comments about each other's physical appearance, such as criticising the ear size or mouth shape. It may be either by teasing or in the form of jokes, but it has some effects on the victim.

Social media platforms where users often present curated, flawlessly edited images, can foster insecurity in some individuals. This can exert undue pressure on others, making them feel inadequate or unattractive in their natural state. Teenagers are also affected seriously as bullies tend to target kids who are obese or too slim or have different looks from others. This affects those being bullied, leading to stressful situations which can lead them to depression.

Some of the effects on those being body-shamed are:

Some will be pressured to undergo risky and expensive plastic surgery procedures to change some of their appearances.

Some will become exercise enthusiasts to maintain a particular shape.

Body shaming can lead to social withdrawal and isolation, causing individuals to disconnect from others and hide their true selves. They believe they are not good enough, which will affect their confidence and self-esteem. All these can lead to a state of anxiety and depression.

SUGGESTIONS:

We need to create awareness of the harmful effects of body shaming.

Parents and carers should equip children with coping skills and resilience to navigate various challenging situations in life.

The focus should be on healthy living, eating good food, exercising, getting enough sleep, and doing things in moderation, rather than focusing on looks.

People should be mindful of the jokes they crack, considering that not everyone is built with strong coping skills to laugh over certain things and move on.

IMPOSTER SYNDROME

It refers to when someone does not feel the absolute joy of success despite excelling in an activity. They do not feel they are competent or talented enough. They are always anxious and fearful that people will discover their inadequacy. Instead of recognising their accomplishments, they tend to focus inward, criticising themselves and dwelling on doubts. It is an issue many people suffer alone, thinking it is peculiar to them.

Some high achievers will eventually begin to doubt their abilities to continue performing at that rate. This can be very stressful for the person involved. When they receive people's admiration, there is always that inward nagging doubt. If not addressed, this can lead to chronic anxiety. Pressure to perform in one way or another tends to lead to imposter syndrome. The family can pressure the children to excel and be critical of any minor mistake. Also, there is pressure to perform and belong to one social group or association. There is a constant quest to make an outstanding achievement that will guarantee a place in the group coupled with the fear that they might not be able to keep up with the achievement.

Some have adopted a negative thought process out of ignorance. They keep talking down on themselves, doubting their abilities, always scared that they will fail. It is a stressful situation and can lead to depression and frustration.

The constant fear, self-sabotage, burnout, and downplaying of contributions significantly impact the person.

SUGGESTIONS:
Self-awareness is crucial.
Identify and change thought patterns from negative thoughts to positive and empowering ones.
Focus on objective facts, rather than emotions or personal feelings.
Practise self-care and cultivate self-compassion.
Therapy.

HUSTLE CULTURE
It is based on the idea that we do all we can to achieve success, even to the detriment of our self-care. Also, our values and self-esteem are tied to our ability to succeed and excel. The relentless quest to be busy and work hard to be successful - which neglects the work-life balance - tends to promote chronic stress in people.

Hustle culture can improve productivity, drive us to excel, and accomplish great things. When it becomes unhealthy, we push ourselves beyond the limit, and other areas of our lives suffer. We neglect other areas of our lives, such as relationships, rest, and personal well-being, and focus all our time and energy on accomplishing great things. With time, our overall health will be impacted.

Hustle culture tends to leave people stressed and can lead to burnout. It affects work-life balance, which is crucial in life. It affects self-esteem, as your achievements and accomplishments are tied to your self-esteem. It increases loneliness and isolation. Burnout resulting from hustle culture may lead to apathy. It affects sleep and will make you prone to anxiety. It causes physical signs like headaches, digestive issues, high blood pressure, etc.

SUGGESTIONS:

Maintain a clear boundary between your work and life balance.

Have clearly defined priorities

Never associate your self-esteem with external things like accomplishments or performance.

Practise self-care.

Acquire good coping skills.

Establish your own definition of success different from what you learn from an influencer on social media, or what some people identify with.

Seek therapy or guidance from trusted people.

NATURAL DISASTERS

A natural disaster is a very devastating and stressful life experience. It causes injuries and loss of life and disrupts the lives of the people affected.

Natural disasters have a profound impact on the mental health of the affected. Many will recover immediately without significant issues, while some will have mental health issues that will continue long after the disaster.

Some effects are difficulty sleeping, sadness, and a sense of loss. There will be fear and anxiety, which may lead to depression. There may be flashbacks and changes in mood and there is also the risk of substance abuse as a coping mechanism.

Children will need help with academic activities. The impact on children depends on their exposure to the disaster, and how the parents or guardians protected and supported them during the tragedy, and the aftermath.

SUGGESTIONS:

Children need to be supported and given a listening ear.

Allow the children to communicate their feelings about the traumatic event.

Do not neglect them; teach them good coping skills necessary to handle such a disaster.

They should be equipped earlier before such an incident happens.

The need for a responsive government that assists and protects the people during crises.

Need to encourage community self-help.

Therapy and practising of self-care.

AGEISM

Discrimination against people because of their age can negatively affect them. Ageism can be directed at oneself, where the person carries a negative attitude about ageing, and has a negative view of oneself owing to one's older age. It can be between two individuals who believe the other is too old to do certain things. This can cause humiliation or frustration on the part of the older one. It can also be systemic, where employers give preference to younger employees.

Some of the effects of ageism are:

It can lead to a sense of worthlessness, which may result in depression.

Some negative comments about ageism can affect their self-esteem.

It causes loneliness and isolation, which may result in cognitive decline, affect sleep patterns, and increase stress levels.

They are at higher risk of being defrauded by scams, which may result in shame and may lead to depression.

SUGGESTIONS:

We need to avoid stereotypes and discrimination against people because of age.

They should be allowed to contribute as much as they can rather than assuming that all of them are no longer needed.

They need good coping skills. They need to handle any challenging moments they may encounter.

Adequate support system is essential.

RETIREMENT

When a person has to stop working and leave his job because of old age, it marks a significant change in their life and has many positive and negative outcomes.

Some positive changes are that they are more relaxed, and their stress level is low due to the removal of work-related pressure. They will spend more time doing leisure activities, travelling, mild exercises, and social engagements.

Some of the negative changes are difficulty in transitioning from work routines to the new reality of not knowing what to do with excess time on their hands, leading to anxiety.

They are isolated from their colleagues and friends at their former places of work and feel they are no longer valuable in society.

Also, the presence of some chronic health challenges

affecting many retirees will affect their mobility, increasing isolation and loneliness, and can lead to many mental health issues.

SUGGESTIONS:

They need a strong support network to navigate during the transition.

They must contact other retirees, friends, and family to avoid loneliness.

They need to create new goals and plans to focus on.

They need to manage both their physical and mental health.

Acceptance of reality or adjusting to the new change in life.

Self-care.

Good coping skills.

ECONOMIC CRISIS

Economic crises affect the citizens of affected countries in different ways. It worsens income inequality and causes a rise in poverty. Many workers will lose their jobs or earn lower pay, affecting their ability to care for themselves and their families. Loss of a job is always a traumatic experience, and the stress will affect one's mental health, resulting in fear, worry, and anxiety. The concern of being unable to pay bills or give their children a quality education, and a good life puts tremendous stress on parents.

Some of the negative consequences of unemployment are:

The dangers of drug or alcohol abuse to cope with the stress involved by numbing the pain experienced.

It may lead to loneliness.

SUGGESTIONS:

The government needs an adequate safety net to provide essential services to citizens during a crisis. This will lessen the stress associated with poverty and unemployment.

People must maintain good communication with family, friends, and their communities as a support base, especially during trying moments.

SUPERSTITIOUS BELIEFS

Superstitious beliefs are beliefs not rooted in fact or logic, but people still believe in them. They may be connected to cultural traditions or religious practices. Some superstitious beliefs can be helpful to a person, or harmful when they distort reality. Some use them to lower stress levels or give them confidence to perform a task well.

It is a form of control of external circumstances not within our actual control and can lead to anxiety and depression. Children may believe in superstitious beliefs more than adults.

SUGGESTIONS:

We need to understand that superstitious beliefs are not rooted in reality.

A robust coping skill is needed, so superstitious people will look for other ways of managing their thought processes.

People need to understand that there are things they can control and cannot.

OPPRESSION

It is the unfair use of power to benefit some people while harming or humiliating others. Oppression is fully present in the world, and it is possible many have experienced the adverse effects of oppression. Some of the pillars of oppression are power and privileges. One group has power over another and can impose their will on them, depriving them of access to many things. This power to influence things over another will give the members of a powerful group more privileges than other members of another group. The majority will control the minorities, and the members will enjoy many privileges through their affiliation. There are different groups in society (sex, race, age, abilities, national origin, etc.).

Some of the power and privileges examples are:

Race: This can be seen in the power dynamics between the white and coloured population in the USA. The whites have the power and are the powerful group in the USA, and they enjoy a lot of privileges by being members of the influential group.

Sex: Men are dominant in the world. They are an influential group, and can influence a lot both in society, as heads of families, and heads of different cultural groups. So, a man enjoys many privileges that women find difficult to enjoy easily. That is why so many laws are imposed in many countries that limit the prospects and freedom of women around the world. Women's groups are trying to change some of the obnoxious policies affecting them. There is always resistance from the male dominant group to grant all. Removing all obstacles will put them at a disadvantage, which means losing those free privileges they enjoy.

Those restrictions and limitations affecting one group alone, and hindering their growth and freedom are evidence of an oppressed group.

Oppression operates in many different forms. It can be oppression between individuals expressed as prejudices, discrimination, and stereotypes.

Oppression can be expressed through policies by institutions and organisations that reinforce those stereotypes, prejudices, and discriminatory behaviour. An example is police officers profiling young black men alone for detailed searches while leaving whites to pass freely. Shooting an unarmed black man just for assuming all black men are dangerous.

Helplessness and inability to confront the oppressive system made some people channel their rage inward and vent their anger on members of their group. This is referred to as Internalised Oppression. They tend to accept the views of the oppressor. They may start looking down on their members.

They absorb the oppressive narrative that their cultural identity, including language, beliefs, traditions, foods, etc., is lesser than others. The effect will trickle down to looking down on their communities, societies, etc. Some individuals may choose to maintain a safe distance or avoid connection with their own community while seeking approval and validation from the dominant group.

SUGGESTIONS:
First and foremost, there is need to accept there is oppression by the dominant group that enjoys power and unearned privileges.

Speaking out against oppression in any form is expedient.

Showing empathy to one another should be embraced.

Strong government policies and laws to stop oppression in all its ways should be established.

Counselling is essential for individuals who have Internalised Oppression to enable them to recognise the harm inflicted upon themselves and others.

PREJUDICE, STEREOTYPE, DISCRIMINATION

People have different experiences, beliefs, and abilities. A stereotype is an unfair or dangerous assumption or negative thought about a person or group. Prejudice is a negative attitude towards a person or group based on a stereotype. Discrimination is an action based on a prejudiced view.

Stereotypes, prejudice, and discrimination continue in our world due to ignorance, false teaching, and a perceived need by perpetrators to conform to the norms. People learn their beliefs from parents, siblings, friends, teachers, media, and society.

A stereotypical view of a person always tags along with the expectation that the person will behave in a certain way that conforms to one's view. The issue stems from the tendency for individuals holding prejudiced views to disregard or discount the positive qualities and actions of the person or group they are biased against. Their attention is drawn to negative information, which reinforces their expectations and perpetuates existing stereotypes.

Victims of prejudice, stereotypes, and discrimination may experience loneliness and isolation. They will have trouble sleeping, have low self-esteem, and are prone to anxiety and depression. They may have problems with academics and may have difficulty trusting others. Many will feel a sense of hopelessness.

SUGGESTIONS:
Need for laws and policies to protect people from discriminating practices.

There is a need for the formation of organisations aimed at putting an end to stereotypes, prejudice, and discrimination.

There is a need for people to avoid the practice, and not support anyone engaging in it.

People need to adopt good coping skills and have self-confidence to reduce the impact of being targeted.

GENDER DISCRIMINATION

This is any action done to exclude people based on gender,

and it may be deliberate or out of ignorance. It can take place in any area of life: in some families, preferences are given to male children; in spiritual organisations, where women are not allowed to play specific roles; in some countries, where women are not allowed to participate in political processes or be in positions of authority; while in other countries, women are not allowed to participate in sports. There are countries where women are not even allowed to go out in public without a man accompanying them. Some women are not allowed to drive, or even use any beauty products.

These systems are extremely stressful for women and will affect their mental health. Some may develop depression and anxiety.

SUGGESTIONS:
Enhanced legislation and policies are crucial to combat discrimination against women.

Greater awareness is urgently needed to address the pervasive harm caused by discrimination against women and its far-reaching implications for society.

SCAMS/FRAUD

Fraud and scams have a devastating impact on the lives of the victims, apart from financial and psychological problems, which can affect the overall life of the victims. The severity depends on the magnitude of the fraud on the individual concerned, and their mental state. It is a severe threat to the people and their families.

Fraudsters devise different ways and means to perpetrate their act.

Romance fraud: They pretend to be in love with the victim, using a fake identity. They tend to target vulnerable women, including single mothers, widows, old, and lonely women. They typically employ manipulative tactics to gain trust, pretending to be caring and supportive to gain their confidence. They shower them with compliments, etc. They usually target victims from social media and dating sites. Some will offer marriage proposals, all in a bid to make the victim think they have found 'The One' Scammers will initiate the extortion process, fabricating urgent needs to deceive victims into sending money. Common ruses include:

1. **Immigration issues:** Claiming to require funds to resolve visa or travel problems to meet the victim.
2. **Medical emergencies:** Falsely alleging severe illnesses or injuries requiring immediate financial assistance.
3. **Business crises:** Pretending to face financial ruin or legal troubles, seeking funds to alleviate the situation.

It is always one form of extortion or the other.

419 (Advance Fee Fraud): A type of advance fee fraud where victims are duped into paying money upfront, expecting to receive a large sum or valuable opportunity, such as a contract, inheritance, etc. They may request your help in getting money from a bank in respect of a dead person whose money is stuck in the bank. There is always a promise that you will get a percentage for your kind gesture.

There are many other ways fraudsters operate, including investment fraud, fake services on the Internet, fake cheques, and job opportunities. Any event, be it the COVID pandemic or natural disasters, is always an avenue to perpetrate fraud on the victim. Some of the means they use are building trust with the victim and creating a sense of urgency.

Common risk factors that increase an individual's vulnerability to fraud include:

Some individuals tend to trust easily, often due to a lack of awareness or understanding of potential risks.

People who are isolated or lonely, probably due to

circumstances like marriage, breakup, financial problems, or loss of loved ones, are prime targets.

Victims who are defrauded face a lot of mental health challenges. Some are ashamed to report to the authorities or notify anyone of the ordeal. They are fearful of being branded greedy and stupid to fall for such. This exacerbates their internal turmoil, intensifying feelings of stress, anger and shame, leading to silent suffering. thereby increasing their stress levels. Many may be depressed and might commit suicide or harm themselves. It affects their behaviours, and this will have an impact on their relationships, too. They will lose confidence in themselves and blame themselves for their action. This will lead to negative self-talk, worsening their mental state.

They suffer a loss of reputation and low self-esteem. Others may face the devastating collapse of their marriage, leading to severe emotional, financial, and social consequences.

SUGGESTIONS:

Be mindful and avoid business opportunities, or requests for help received via email from unknown senders.

Before signing any contract, conduct due diligence, investigate thoroughly, and consider consulting a professional to review and verify its terms.

People must be careful about the products or services they want to buy online.

People should not click on a link from any mail that is not from a trusted organisation.

They must be careful of information posted online because fraudsters use that information to target their victims.

Never respond to emails informing you that you won a prize or lottery when you know you have never applied for any competition or lottery.

People should be careful when dating on sites and divulging personal information to people they do not know online.

They should not part with money to anyone they do not know personally (one-on-one).

Victims should be supported, not shamed or blamed for being gullible.

Public awareness campaigns should encompass all forms of fraud, prioritising education and support for susceptible populations (vulnerable groups).

RELATIONSHIPS

This is a connection between people and how they feel and behave towards one another. It can be an emotional relationship between two people in a marriage or friendship. In terms of human relationships, a healthy relationship is equally beneficial to the two people involved. It is filled with happiness and joy, and there is no manipulation of one by another. For a relationship to work perfectly, the two partners must agree to make it work. It requires time, commitment, sacrifice, and compassion to make it work. When two people from different backgrounds and experiences come together as a team, there are bound to be differences as both cannot always think alike. This is where sacrifice is required. In any partnership, it is unrealistic to expect one person to always get their way while the other simply follows. This dynamic inevitably leads to conflicts and issues.

Numerous challenges can transform a healthy relationship into a toxic one. Some of these challenges include:

Infidelity: Infidelity severely damages the bond in a relationship, causing profound emotional pain and hurt to the betrayed partner. It may be sexual or flirting. It breaks the trust in the relationship and can lead to its dissolution.

Parenting: Taking care of children is challenging if the partners disagree on a parenting style whereby one partner leaves the responsibility of the child's upbringing to the other, leading to pressure. It will eventually lead to problems. People like to be appreciated and complimented on the efforts they make in building the relationship. If neglected, they will lose interest, and the relationship may end.

Life changes can impact a relationship. If the partners' sex life is fantastic, fun, and wild, and after a while, one of them starts to experience low libido, it is bound to create problems. Also, people can change their plans about life as they grow and have more experience. Consider a couple who previously enjoyed a lavish lifestyle, frequently attending parties and showcasing their wealth. If one partner suddenly decides to adopt a more modest lifestyle, it can create significant conflict and tension in the relationship.

Poor communication among the partners can create severe problems in the relationship. Some partners assume their significant other will intuitively understand their feelings without open communication. However, this is very difficult. Also, some need to learn how to resolve conflicts amicably. Some partners will insist on getting their way in every dispute. Consequently, this attitude poses a significant problem which will lead the couple to start growing emotionally apart.

Finances are one of the most significant issues in relationships. If there is no mutually agreed-upon plan earlier on how to spend money, it wreaks havoc on the relationship. When one partner is a spontaneous spender, drawn to the latest gadgets and fashion trends, while the other is more frugal and cautious, conflicts are likely to arise.

Also, having a joint account by couples is another big challenge. The couple who brings in more than the other will naturally expect the other to increase their contribution. It is worse when the woman is bringing more than the husband. It will make the man feel less and may affect his self-esteem. Men are naturally expected to be the breadwinner; if the man does not make more than the wife, he will feel pressure. Some women may be understanding, but some may snap at him during any conflict, reminding him that she is the person who foots the significant bill. In such cases, the man will feel defeated and humiliated.

Taking each other for granted is another relationship issue if handled poorly. As partners grow together, the initial spark often fades gradually. They begin to see each other's true selves. They may start doing things without notifying their partner. This creates little friction in the partnership until it explodes into more significant problems.

Being jealous in a relationship is very dangerous due to some people's past experiences in life or even previous relationships. They learn some unhealthy coping skills. This will lead them to cling to their partner demanding attention on themselves alone. This harmful behaviour will even lead them to compare their partner's relationship to their family, friends, etc. The jealousy may lead some to try to end their partner's warm and supportive relationship with siblings, friends, or parents. When their partner receives visits from loved ones, such as parents or friends, they become uncomfortable and tend to interrupt conversations, indicating underlying insecurities.

A wild and dangerous lifestyle can negatively impact the relationship when a partner becomes addicted to a lifestyle, such as drugs/alcohol or even orgies, and then attempts to coerce or manipulate the other partner into participating.

External influences can wreak havoc on a relationship. Some partners present their challenges to trusted family members, friends, or religious leaders. These people need to be entirely on the ground to know the actual issue between the couple; they act based on advice from one to suggest a solution for how they will handle their partners. Most often, those solutions tend to worsen the relationship as some are based on one-sided information.

There are partners with severe behavioural problems, like narcissists, psychopaths, and sadists. Any relationship with any of these is bound to be disastrous, no matter how good, nice, or understanding the other partner is. Sadists derive pleasure from others' pain, so, they enjoy how their partners suffer in the relationship. They are always hostile, lack empathy, lack responsibilities, and love violence. They want to use their power over a powerless victim. In such a relationship, one can do nothing to change the person. It is who they are. They need help, and since their partners are not therapists and remain in that relationship, they may end up as emotional wrecks. They may suffer severe mental health issues, or even die in the process. A similar issue will arise if someone has a psychopath as a partner. They resemble the sadist in many ways.

Narcissists always have problems in relationships. They believe they are unique. Anything they do is for their benefit alone. They love to be worshipped but will look down on their partner. They have a sense of entitlement and love to belittle people. They live in a world of illusion where they believe they are essential and everything they do is excellent and valuable. They are not comfortable with criticism. So, having a narcissist as a partner is challenging. Any conflict resolution skill or reasoning one uses to try and rationalise things will not work.

SUGGESTIONS:
Individuals need to know that some relationship

problems cannot be solved with their partner, for example, having a sadist, psychopath, or narcissist as a partner. So, there is no need to take it personally or blame themselves for problems in that relationship.

Always take responsibility and make amends if you are at fault.

There is a need for partners to show empathy towards one another.

Seeking counselling when necessary.

Need for all to express gratitude and compliment and commend one another.

Keep the channel of communication open regardless of the problem.

Couples must decide on their financial goals, and whether a joint or separate account is appropriate. Taking into cognizance that what works for one couple might not work for another.

It is essential to avoid external influences.

There is a need to strike a balance in communication with in-laws. One partner's family and friends should not have free access, and the other's family and friends are not allowed the same degree of access. This will lead to problems.

IMPACT OF STRESS AT DIFFERENT LIFE STAGES

CHILDHOOD

Stress is a normal part of life. So, any situation that requires the child to adapt to a new behaviour can be stressful. Some stress can be considered positive when it is necessary for the development and growth of the child, however, some can negatively affect their mental and physical health.

There are many causes of stress in children which include:

Divorce/Separation: This is a very stressful period for the children as they adjust to their new situation.

Death: The death of a parent or loved one can adversely affect the child.

Bullying: Bullying by siblings, and in school is always a stressful moment for the child.

Domestic Violence: Children who witness domestic violence between their parents tend to suffer stress more than those in homes free from violence.

Relationship: The pressure to maintain relationships with peers, coupled with pressure to belong within their peer groups can be stressful for the child as well.

Parental Expectation: Parents' pressure to perform well and excel in their academics puts serious pressure on children.

Parenting Style: A poor parenting style that is authoritative or neglectful can be stressful to children.

Domestic abuse by parents or caregivers in terms of beating and deprivation of food as a means of punishment could be stressful for the children.

Poverty and its associated issues, homelessness, and poor housing are severe stressors to children.

Moving to a new place is initially stressful too.

Periods of war or displacement or natural disasters have a stressful impact on children.

Some of the signs of stress in children:

Younger children tend to be clingy to their parents or caregivers.

They tend to become more demanding and cry very often.

Their sleeping and eating patterns change.

They become fearful and withdrawn.

They may bed wet.

For Older Children:

They will have concentration problems and difficulty focusing on a task.

They become fearful and withdrawn.

They experience changes in sleeping patterns.

They may complain of stomach pain or other disturbances without being sick.

They may experience nightmares.

They may be aggressive or act out.

Also, they may experience general body aches, weight changes, dizziness, and shortness of breath.

They may have difficulty controlling their emotions, which can be in the form of rebellion.

Managing children's stress is the responsibility of parents and adults. Parents ought to teach their children how to read, write, etc., and guide them in managing their emotions, and the stresses they witness. Often, children's behaviours are a way of seeking attention from their parents or caregivers. Children need a safe, controlled, and loving environment to thrive. They need the love and support from parents and caregivers to grow up with good coping skills to deal with any stress they may have encountered.

Parents play a crucial role in recognising their child's stress and equipping them with techniques to handle it. By doing so, the child gains a better understanding of their environment and learns how to handle challenging situations. Parents should set a good example of how to handle stressful situations in their own lives.

Children learn behaviours and attitudes from their parents more than what they say by mouth. Parents and caregivers should encourage the children to have positive feelings about themselves, whilst they seek solutions, and not focus on problems or negativity.

Encourage healthy living so the children can develop healthy habits towards time to eat, exercise, play with friends, and rest. Also, they must practise mindfulness and focus only on the present moment.

Parents should boost their children's confidence and self-esteem by complimenting and praising them when they perform well and discussing how to improve when they make mistakes. This way, they will get to know that mistakes are part of learning. Parents should monitor the programs their children watch and restrict their access to social media.

Parents should ensure good communication with their

children. They should listen and validate their fears; instead of lecturing them, they should allow the children the liberty to explore and make mistakes in a controlled manner.

They should seek help if they notice any severe disturbance in their wards.

ADOLESCENCE

Stress is always part of human life, and teenagers will experience stress from time to time. It helps their growth and development, but chronic stress will affect their everyday lives. So, it is crucial to create awareness to enable teenagers to identify stress early on and know how to cope with it.

There are many causes of teenage stress:

Divorce/Separation: This situation affects teenagers in the home, and the stress they experience will also affect their other lives in school and their relationships. The way the parents handle separation/divorce will also impact their lives.

Bullying: This is one of the greatest dangers faced by teenagers. Bullying is very stressful for them in school. However, cyberbullying is another level of bullying that impacts their lives a lot. The audience for social media is vast compared to bullying witnessed only within a particular environment.

Parental Expectation: Parents' pressure on teens puts a lot of stress on them. The pressure to excel, get admitted to elite universities, and excel in sports can have a profound impact on teenagers' mental well-being.

Poverty and inequality, homelessness, and other things associated with poverty tend to put stress on the teens experiencing such situations.

Social Situations: Some teens suffer from low self-esteem and confidence due to how their parents train them.

Maintaining friendships is an ordeal.

Work/Study: Some teens combine work, study, and sports. Balancing these responsibilities is not easy for them.

Peer Pressure: Teenagers face constant pressure to conform to their peers' expectations, fearing social exclusion or seeking acceptance within popular groups. Some will be under pressure to bully other students and will either join in bullying or encourage bullies to avoid falling out with their peer group. Some will be under pressure to drink or smoke to blend in too. All these and more put them under stressful situations. The hormonal changes they undergo are also stressful for them.

Negative self-talk: Some teens engage in negative self-talk and feel they are not good enough; they criticise and judge themselves based on minor issues. This self-talk and its attendant negative thoughts will put them under stress.

Relationships: Romantic relationship challenges encountered are another stressful period in their life. Arguments with friends can result in stressful moments. Teenagers who are disabled will have additional stress to handle, apart from the everyday stress their peers go through due to their vulnerability.

Some of the signs of stress in teens:

The teen starts to withdraw from some hobbies or hanging out with friends.

They tend to get quickly angry, anxious, or tearful. This may include walking out while their parents are still talking to them or banging on doors.

A change in their eating habits or sleeping patterns occurs. Either they overeat, or they need to eat more.

Their academic performance starts to drop.

They may complain of aches and pains.

They need help concentrating and may need help to

remember their daily house chores or tasks.

They may start using alcohol/drugs, whilst indulging in risky behaviours like partying and risky sexual activities.

They may suffer from depression and would prefer to be left alone.

They begin to feel sad and hopeless.

SUGGESTIONS:

Parents and guardians need to teach teenagers about stress management so they can cope with it.

Parents should teach them about what is in their power to control, and what is not. This is one of the primary reasons people need not be more stressed.

Parents should create a safe and non-judgmental space for their teenagers to express their feelings freely, without pressure, and at their own pace.

This is not the time for lectures. Instead, listen as your teen shares their experiences, stresses, and coping strategies.

Parents need to teach their teens good coping skills and lead by example.

Parents should stop placing undue pressure on teens to perform well.

Motivate them and encourage them to be the best they can be. Whatever the outcome, support them to keep doing their best, and ensure that failure or mistakes are part of learning, not used for mocking or putting them down.

Teenagers need to build a network of supportive and positive-minded friends.

They should adopt a healthy lifestyle.

Teenagers need to avoid negative self-talk; they should switch negative thought patterns with positive ones.

They should maintain healthy boundaries and learn when to say no to unhealthy behaviours or requests.

Parents should spend adequate time with their teens.

Listen to them and do some activities together.

Teenagers should make time for relaxation and quality time with friends and families.

They should reduce the time they spend on social media. They need to know that what they see posted are idealised versions of people, so, they should not allow it to affect their self-esteem.

Also, they need to know that social media was built to be addictive, so once you are online, you are hooked.

Teenagers also need to know that they should not allow people's behaviour or attitudes to affect their lives. They have the choice of being happy or sad, and no one can make them happy or sad without their consent. So, they will live life at their own pace and not based on someone else's idea of what a good life should be.

They need to get help, when necessary, either through counselling or talking with someone they trust.

They must learn that bullying in all its forms is not good or cool. They should not participate in, support, or watch where it is being perpetrated.

ADULTHOOD

Stress is a normal part of life, but chronic stress can cause significant harm to our mental health. In adults, chronic stress can result in adverse mental, physical, and behavioural problems. The intensity of stress experienced by an adult depends on their coping skills and level of exposure to the stressors. Stress has both positive and negative aspects. It will help you focus and meet challenges, but chronic stress can cause damage. It affects the quality of life of the individual.

Both internal and external factors can cause stress. Ruminating, negative self-talk and thoughts are internal stressors. External stressors are numerous situations that can put pressure on an individual. An individual who has a negative view of life is worried about how things will turn out and is always thinking about the worst, so will always be under pressure. The same is true of the person who finds it challenging to accept change and is always scared of any change they might encounter.

Some of the causes of stress in adulthood are:

Family: Training the children is always stressful for the parents considering that they are two different individuals from different backgrounds, with different views about parenting. They must navigate how to relate with their respective in-laws and siblings. This may cause problems due to interference from one family or the other in the couple's affairs.

Relationship: Maintaining a healthy and robust relationship takes sacrifice and effort. There will always be some challenges in the relationship. One person's idea of a relationship may differ from the other. Some may want to start a family, while others may need more preparation time. One partner may prefer a joint account for everything as a team, but the other prefers a bit of independence. All these issues tend to put pressure on the relationship. Additionally, some may likely be in a relationship with a narcissist, which can be devastating.

Work/School: Challenges faced in the workplace are a significant source of pressure on an individual; the pressure to meet deadlines, work-related gossip, and politics. If the job is not fulfilling, it will impact their mental health. Those running their businesses face the challenges and pressures of raising funds, marketing, and competing with other firms. The pressure is always intense to ensure the company survives and succeeds.

Job Loss: Job loss is a very stressful period, coupled with fear of how to pay bills and the challenge of another job hunt.

Death: The death of a loved one is unfortunate, and a distressing moment. It is very stressful trying to come to terms with the loss.

Sickness: If a close loved one has a chronic or terminal illness, it can also put pressure on an individual.

Financial Problems are one of the leading causes of problems in a relationship. They may lead to arguments and quarrels about how to spend money collectively.

Social media: Some adults put undue pressure on themselves to live up to the expectations and standards of the people they see on social media. Also, some are addicted to social media with its attendant consequences on their mental health.

Retirement: Some adults retire early. The change from work mode to having too much time on their hands tends to create pressure on them to fill their days with activities. Also, the loss of social contact in their workplace will make them feel a sense of loss in the early stages of their retirement.

Some of the signs of chronic stress in adults are:

They focus on the negative, and are always in a state of worry, even over meaningless things.

They ruminate a lot and are always anxious.

They have problems concentrating, and memory problems.

They tend to be moody, and easily irritated.

They feel sad.

They withdraw from people.

They feel overwhelmed and helpless.

They have sleeping problems and either eat more, or less.

They tend to procrastinate.

They get restless and may be involved in drug or alcohol

abuse.

SUGGESTIONS:

Stress management and coping skills are essential.

Practise mindfulness and meditation.

Adopt healthy living - eat good meals, exercise, relax, and take vacations.

They must spend time with loved ones, family, friends, and others.

They need to adopt a work-life balance and have clearly defined boundaries.

They should set realistic, achievable goals and focus on enjoying the process of accomplishing them.

Limit the time spent on social media, or any digital medium.

Effective communication is essential between partners.

Parents should adopt a mutually agreed parenting style for their children.

Those in a relationship should ensure that there is no external interference.

They should learn that there are things within their control and accept them in good faith.

They should refrain from trying to change others and embrace their authenticity.

OLD ADULTHOOD

Older adults are amongst the vulnerable groups and are also exposed to stress like everyone else. Also, in addition, they may be facing one chronic health challenge or the other, which is another form of stress.

Some of the causes of stress for older adults are:

Retirement: Retirement affects the older adults in a lot of ways. They tend to lose the identity they have built up over the years owing to their work designation.

They suffer isolation as they are no longer in contact with their colleagues.

They have so much time on their hands and do not know how to fill the hours, so some of these factors put a lot of stress on them as they try to figure out what to do with their lives.

Loneliness is a significant problem for older adults; they are no longer working, and their children have moved on with their families. They are left alone; some may be in a nursing home or in their homes alone.

The sense of isolation and boredom affects their mental well-being.

Chronic illness: The pains and financial cost involved in treating their health condition is a significant burden on them.

Financial problem: Many need more funds to cover their expenses, including the rising medical bills.

Dependence: Due to weakness or other health challenges, they depend on others to assist them do some basic things, such as cleaning the house, cooking, etc.

The feeling of being dependent on someone for things they used to do on their own tends to weigh them down. Due to health constraints, they are left with no choice but to rely on others, sacrificing their independence. Not being able to do certain things independently is a frustrating experience for them.

Loss of family or a spouse affects them leading to more feelings of loneliness and isolation.

Carers: They may be abused by caregivers in nursing homes or their own homes.

Caretaking demand: Some older adults may find themselves taking care of their spouses at an advanced age, which puts extra pressure on them due to their weak state.

Some of the signs of stress include:
Finding it difficult to sleep.
They may feel tired.
They may have poor concentration.
They may have changes in bowel movement.
Headaches and pains all over the body.
They might experience a change in appetite.
They are at risk of depression.
Withdrawal from people.
They may have poor judgment.
Constant worry and general unhappiness.
They may have problems with hygiene.

SUGGESTIONS:
Children and caregivers need to limit things that will be a source of stress for older adults.

There would be a need for constant visits and phone calls or video chats.

Teaching older adults about stress management and good coping skills:

Encourage them to have new hobbies, try new activities, and join some support groups so they will be in contact with others to avoid loneliness.

Practise healthy living by eating well, exercising, and getting adequate sleep.

They need to practise mindfulness meditation as their strength permits them.

They should be encouraged to focus on things they can control and leave the ones out of their control.

CHAPTER 3

EMOTIONS AS SIGNALS

ANGER

Anger is an essential emotion when managed appropriately. However, it becomes a problem when mismanaged.

It can motivate us to make significant changes in our lives and can equally be destructive because it is a powerful emotion; it can result in serious relationship problems like arguments and can lead to fights and even murder.

The causes of anger issues are numerous. The way people are brought up plays a significant role in their lives. Some learn to express their anger violently to get what they want, probably because of what they observed when they were young. Some tend to bottle up their anger and suppress it because they fear how it can be perceived. This unresolved issue can lead to explosive outrage at any time.

Some people tend to overreact to certain situations based on their past experiences. People who have been disregarded or dismissed in the past may feel vulnerable in a group setting, driven by a desire for acknowledgement rather than resentment. Their anger and hurt make them lash out, convinced of intentional disregard. This emotional response prevents them from considering other perspectives.

People can be angry at situations they may encounter, such as discrimination or injustice. The loss of loved ones can also make us feel angry. Problems in government and society can fill people with anger, causing people's outrage at politicians.

When people are facing health challenges, they can become angry if they are not getting the proper treatment or even adequate support from loved ones. Hunger and lack of sleep can also make us prone to anger at the slightest moment.

Some mental health disorders and substance abuse are also possible causes of anger issues.

There are some health challenges associated with anger, which are caused by constant high stress levels in our system when we are dealing with anger issues. Some of them are high blood pressure, insomnia, stroke, heart attack, headache, and digestive problems.

Some of the emotional symptoms of anger issues are irritability, stress, frustration, anger, etc.

People express anger in various ways. Some individuals direct their anger inward, manifesting it as talking negatively to themselves, they may also try to isolate themselves. Some express anger at other people, animals, or objects by cursing, kicking, or even shooting someone during arguments. Some express anger indirectly, like using silent treatment, not talking to others or sulking.

People need to express anger healthily for optimal emotional well-being. They need to understand that anger is a normal emotion and that they do not need to obey its command.

They should know that the emotion tells them something is happening that they dislike, so, they need to review it consciously and take positive action.

Anger may indicate that we have compromised and are angry with ourselves. It may remind you that someone is crossing your boundary. You may not be appreciated by your family or at work for what you are doing. When you observe and probe the emotion, you can understand where it is coming from and take positive instead of adverse action.

SUGGESTIONS:

Some people who cannot control their anger can go for anger management counselling to learn how to understand their emotions well.

Need for therapy.

They need to understand what they can control.

FEAR

Fear is the body's warning system. It is present in all human beings for protection. It is a powerful emotion that notifies us of danger or if we are in harm's way. Fear protects us from danger but can be problematic if improperly handled. It is there for our survival.

Fear helps keep us safe by alerting us about the danger we may encounter, so, we should make wise decisions and avoid them. Without fear, we will not be aware of risk and end up putting ourselves in harm's way. Fear helps us make significant life changes and will alert us to something that will pose a danger in the world, motivating us to do something about it.

Fear helps you focus on what is essential in your life. The fear of losing a loved one will make us make time to bond with them. Also, the fear of losing our job or position will make us focus on being productive and setting a good example.

The fear that one can die at any moment will make us value time, live our lives to the fullest, and avoid procrastination.

Some of the situations and things that can cause a fear response are:

Upbringing – we learn a lot of behaviours from our family and others when we are children. We can learn to fear specific situations from the coping skills we learned in childhood and carry on into adulthood, so, this can make us fear certain things like snakes, spiders, being alone, etc.

Traumatic situations can make us fear specific experiences like a drowning experience, which makes us scared of swimming. Being assaulted at night or in a lonely park will create fear and anxiety when it is dark or in a place that is lonely when people are not around.

Change and uncertainty: The fear of change/ uncertainty affects many people, but to some, it is exciting as a change signals growth and development to them. Past experiences can create fear in people when they face new challenges. Past sad relationships may develop a fear of breaking up in a person's current relationship. This may push them to behave in a way that may jeopardise the present relationship. People who experience crises in the past, like loss of job and income, may become fearful of the future and may have a scarcity mindset. This is a way to prepare for another crisis in the future. It affects their lives.

Some of the effects of fear on physical health include immune and endocrine system dysfunction, sleep problems, eating disorders, headaches, body aches, etc.

It impacts the mental health in many ways. It can lead to mood swings, obsessive-compulsive disorder, anxiety, and feelings of helplessness.

We must understand that fear is a body's normal response and is there for our protection and safety. We must manage and use it for our benefit instead of letting it go out of control and become problematic by affecting our emotional well-being. People need to be curious to understand the message the emotion is trying to tell us. Then, we will respond positively for our benefit and growth. People must practise positive thinking and always look for solutions instead of focusing on problems. Excessive focus on problems will heighten the fear response.

SUGGESTIONS:

There is a need for a support system to help people manage their fears.

People need to learn to replace negative and fearful thoughts with positive and beneficial ones to live healthy lives.

Seek therapy when necessary.

SADNESS

Sadness is an emotional state of unhappiness and low mood. It can be mild, moderate, or extreme. Sadness can serve as a mild alert for self-reflection.

Sadness can help people review their lives, examine what went wrong, and put themselves in that state. They can then consider the solution and find ways of resolving the situation. Thus, such a situation can improve their motivation to do the right thing.

Sadness helps elicit empathy. When we see someone sad and crying, we naturally want to understand what makes them unhappy and help them.

Children use sadness to show their distress and to elicit help and comfort from parents or caregivers.

Sadness can be dangerous if it is not managed well and is

intense and chronic, it can lead to depression.

Many experiences in life can lead people to be sad:

Death: The death of loved ones can cause sadness as they grieve and mourn the loss.

Self-talk: Self-talk can make someone sad. The person continues to talk to himself negatively, criticising everything and blaming themselves for things happening in their life. They will naturally be down and in a sad state during that moment.

Sickness: This can make people sad as they are battling pain associated with their illness. Being isolated because of sickness or being unable to afford treatment can make the person very sad about the situation. Also, receiving a diagnosis of chronic or terminal illness can put the person in a state of sadness.

School: Not performing to expectations in academics or sports or being bullied in school can make an individual sad.

Home: Witnessing domestic violence in the house, either as a victim or observing it, can make the person sad. Also, suffering abuse either by parental neglect or by caregivers can make a child unhappy.

Divorce/Separation can make the partners sad, as their lives will never be the same. The children will also be unhappy about the breakup of their parent's marriage.

Sadness causes individuals to have a low mood, and decreased confidence. They will be unhappy and in a mourning state. They feel low energy, worthlessness, and social withdrawal. They may have trouble sleeping and like to be left alone.

Some physical signs include drooping eyes, slumped posture, and increased or decreased heart rate.

SUGGESTIONS:
People need to be aware of things they can control and

cannot.

There is a need to self-reflect to discover the reason for the sad feelings, and how to resolve the situation causing them, thus coming out better and stronger.

Individuals must reach out to their support system (Family, friends etc.) when they are down. Isolation of themselves will make the situation worse.

JOY

Joy is a state of mind that is not dependent on any circumstance, whether good or bad. Living a life of joy is what every individual can aspire to and look forward to. Joy does not depend on external circumstances; it is internal, so the individual does not need any situation or event to be joyful. Joy comes from the heart and soul. Joy brings peace to the mind and body. Joy helps us to focus on the present moment. Focusing on the present tends to shut down our fears and worries about the future, so, we focus on the present moment and enjoy it fully.

Joy helps improve our health. Being happy and positive lowers our stress levels and blood pressure, which helps to protect us against cardiovascular disease. Joy also helps us make others feel good. When we are in a positive mood, it affects the people around us and attracts people to us. People naturally like to be around someone joyful, and not sad.

Being joyful will also improve our chances of living long. Joy has numerous benefits, so individuals must allow themselves to experience the joy already within them.

SUGGESTIONS:
Individuals must limit negative behaviour and spend more time with positive and joyful people.

They need to develop a mindset that makes joyful living a norm.

They need to practise mindfulness/meditation, which will help them be present in the moment.

Helping others in the community helps bring more joy to life.

They need to pursue new plans and projects that give purpose to their lives. Practising self-care and living a healthy life will bring us more joy.

SURPRISE

This happens when we encounter an unexpected movement or sound and try to understand what is happening. It always occurs within a very short period. Depending on what happened, we may be amused, angry, fearful, or disgusted following the event.

Surprises can be positive, making the individual look forward to such experiences. They will also share the surprises with others as a form of entertainment. Also, it can be damaging when we receive shocking news. In rare cases, it can lead to the death of someone who may suffer a heart attack as his loved one pulled a surprise birthday party for them, unaware of the plan—for example, hiding in the house and when the person enters the house before putting on the light. There will be a happy birthday shout-out from loved ones, and the light comes on instantly. So, the intense shock can put undue stress on a vulnerable individual, leading to a heart attack.

It can also create fear in some people because it may cause them to react embarrassingly during the surprising moment.

Surprises can lead to a stressful period during a brief event, which may harm some individuals. Surprise helps us accept uncertainty and not be afraid of change, which is good for our well-being. Also, it helps people overcome the fear of being vulnerable in life, as surprise can expose people's vulnerability.

SUGGESTIONS:

People should be mindful of others before surprising them to avoid some unexpected consequences resulting from the surprising moment.

SHAME

Shame arises from the perception of doing something that does not align with our morals and values. It may be immoral or improper. When it becomes chronic, these negative feelings make us feel inadequate or flawed.

Shame helps us survive and conform to cultural and traditional norms. It helps us obey the law or behave humanely. Shame results from dissatisfaction, self-hatred, and doubt. It can be a short-lived event or occur over a long period and become chronic. It may be due to our beliefs about our flaws rather than people's perceptions.

Some causes of shame are:

An individual who sets a very high and unreachable expectation and cannot reach the standard will feel shame.

An individual who is bullied in public will feel a sense of shame and a tendency to be withdrawn.

Individuals excluded from peers or rejected from a group they want to belong to will feel unloved and ashamed.

Shame can also result from parenting styles when they were not adequately loved and trained to have good coping skills.

An individual who is suffering from existing mental health conditions can feel a sense of separation from others due to their condition. This situation can result in an experience of shame.

Some of the effects of shame are:

The person will have low esteem due to negative feelings

of being unworthy of acceptance.

There will be a feeling of emptiness.

They will seek perfection in everything they do to avoid shame or humiliation, which will put undue pressure on them.

They will have relationship issues; they want to please people to their detriment or withdraw from people.

They may experience anxiety due to shame and self-doubt.

It can lead the individual to severe addictions like drugs, alcohol, sex, and unhealthy ways of coping with experiences. It may lead them to exhibit a superiority complex to mask their low esteem; it makes it harder to trust people and avoid some communication to avoid saying something wrong.

It may lead to sadness and depression.

SUGGESTIONS:

People need to learn that there are things they can control and things they cannot control.

They should focus on what they can do to improve their lives in the present moment and avoid focusing on past events.

They should be compassionate with themselves and avoid negative self-talk and criticism.

They should accept mistakes and errors as necessary parts of growing up and learn from them. They are not things to be ashamed of.

They should listen to and understand their emotions, then focus on finding solutions to create a more peaceful and fulfilling life.

They should also seek support from family, friends, or professionals.

REGRET

Regret is a form of counterfactual thinking. It is a part of life, and it is an emotion focused on what we have done and wish it could have been better and different. There are two forms of regret: we regret what we did not do and what we did, including our errors and mistakes.

Regret may be good when it helps us learn from past mistakes and avoid similar mistakes in the future. It helps create pathways for better actions and choices. Anytime a decision is to be made, there is a tendency to experience regret. This is where regret becomes problematic, because once decisions have been made, regret may become counterproductive. The best option is to wait for the outcome and respond appropriately.

Why some people are more prone to regrets:

Uncertainty: Nothing is guaranteed in life. Some people fear uncertainty or change, so, making difficult decisions is always a problem for them. They will always regret their decisions, wishing they had done better instead of accepting the fact that life is unpredictable.

Some individuals fear change, thus when faced with choices that could bring a change in their circumstances, they often hesitate, fearing the potential consequences. If they do take the leap, the chances of regret are always high.

When we are faced with multiple options, we are more likely to regret our choice. People who have very high standards and want everything to be perfect are more prone to regret.

People reflect on decisions they make personally if they go wrong. They do not deeply regret the decisions made by others, even though they might not be happy about the decisions.

During self-reflection, people often regret recent choices. However, when looking back on the distant past, they tend to regret the choices they did not make even more. People are more likely to regret not choosing a particular career, not contesting an election, not starting their own business, or not making peace with their dead loved ones.

Some of the impacts of regret are:

It can lead to poor self-esteem.

It can lead to helplessness.

It can lead to symptoms of anxiety and depression.

It can lead to changes in sleep patterns.

It can affect appetite.

It can cause body pain and headaches.

Also, the fear of regret can cause some people to lack self-confidence. They tend to lose self-confidence. They seek external validation to confirm their decisions.

SUGGESTIONS:

People need to accept themselves, know that mistakes are part of growth, and embrace them instead of being fearful.

They need to know that life is unpredictable and will not always turn out favourably for them.

People must practise mindfulness and avoid rumination and negative self-talk, which help regret flourish.

People should learn good coping skills to thrive and take responsibility for their actions.

People should cultivate self-compassion and develop empathy towards others.

CHAPTER 4

SELF-DESTRUCTIVE BEHAVIOURS AND SUICIDE

SELF-DESTRUCTIVE BEHAVIOURS

This is when a person takes an action capable of harming themselves physically or mentally. Despite potential awareness of the consequences, the person may struggle to control their behaviour. It may be a poor coping mechanism to deal with unresolved pain or discomfort. It may be a way to numb or distract themselves from emotional pain and stressful situations.

Numerous factors can put a person at risk of self-destructive behaviours.

The following are some and their effects on the person:

Spirit, mind, and body misalignment:

When a person's mind and body are not in alignment with the spirit, there will be confusion, making the person weaker. A sense of doubt, indecision, uncertainty, and discomfort tend to fill the gap, causing stress to the person. The spirit in this context refers to spiritual beliefs, morals, and values depending on the individual's belief system. The person might think of doing something unacceptable to his spirit (moral values). The disconnect causes disturbance and stress to the person and may be intense. This can put the person at risk of a mental health disorder, which is a severe risk factor for self-destructive behaviour. Also, the person may indulge in some unhealthy lifestyles like alcohol and substance abuse, etc, to numb those pains or distract themselves. This propels self-destructive behaviours.

MENTAL HEALTH DISORDER

People who have underlying mental health disorders are always prone to serious risk of getting involved in many self-destructive behaviours. They are not able to control their thoughts and actions.

Loneliness: loneliness can expose someone to mental health conditions such as depression. This can even put the person at risk of suicide, alcohol, and substance abuse, etc.

Perfectionism: A person trying to be absolutely perfect in everything is always at risk of chronic stress, which can lead to self-destructive behaviours. Falling short of an idealised image can lead to self-blame and self-criticism.

False teaching: People tend to carry many false teachings in their lives, like the concept of hustle culture. This affects work-life balance and creates stress, which is a risk factor for mental health conditions, and puts people at risk of self-destructive behaviour.

Burnout from work is another stress trigger that will push the person into self-destructive behaviour.

Coping skills: A lack of good coping skills will always put a person at a disadvantage. People who are stressed, having difficulty sleeping, or have stress or headaches may decide to use sleeping pills and pain relievers. They may do this to avoid the stigma attached to mental health issues and going for therapy. Along the line, the person becomes addicted to sleeping pills and other pain medications.

Ignorance: Some people who are ignorant about certain things in life are also at risk of self-destructive behaviour. Some are unaware that true happiness, self-worth, and confidence lie within them. They have accepted the idea of seeking external support to be fully happy or feel good about themselves.

Some have become obsessed with social media as a way to feel good by liking, sharing, following, etc. leading them to indulge in many self-destructive behaviours in the quest for people's acceptance. This may lead to overhyping of achievement, lies about their lives, and addiction to the internet.

Comparison: Some people have low self-esteem and view success or praise of another as a dent in their self-esteem. They feel happy when complimented and praised, but they become unhappy if someone else receives the same recognition. These unhealthy attitudes cause some of them to engage in self-destructive behaviours like alcohol and substance abuse. This is to numb the stress, jealousy, and envy within themselves. It may even lead some to attempt suicide because of depression when they believe they cannot meet up with others.

Peer/ Societal Pressure: Some people get involved in self-destructive behaviours like alcohol and substance abuse due to pressure from their peers or society to belong. Some men believe that engaging in womanising translates to being man enough and a player. Some abuse drugs and alcohol to belong to their group and avoid being left behind.

Trauma: Unresolved trauma can put people at risk of mental health conditions, which results in several self-destructive behaviours.

SUGGESTIONS:

People need to learn good coping skills as early as possible in childhood to help them cope in life. This will enable them to avoid several self-destructive behaviours.

Stress management is needed so that people can learn to regulate their emotions and behaviours.

There is a need for mindfulness practice. Therapy is needed in some cases to help people who are having challenges with their mental health.

SUICIDE

Suicide is taking one's life due to the hopeless feeling of facing a painful and stressful life situation. Individuals struggling with suicidal thoughts often believe that their death is the only way to escape the overwhelming emotional pain they're experiencing; they want the pain to end. So, without the pain they are feeling, they will not commit suicide. Suicide is a preventable death, but a lot of factors and circumstances cause some people to consider it as the final solution to their painful situation.

Before the suicide itself, they are already in a vulnerable period when some signs may be glaring:

Some have problems with concentration.

They are settling their affairs, like giving out some properties or specifying how they want to be buried.

Some may withdraw from family and friends, and others.

There may be some changes in their eating habit or sleeping patterns.

The feeling of hopelessness and feeling trapped in the situation without hope of resolution.

Numerous situations can push some people into suicide or attempt suicide:

Loss of a loved one.

Mental health conditions.

Abuse like bullying or social media abuse.

Financial problems.

Chronic stress.

A painful medical condition.

Family history of suicide or mental disorder.

Having access to guns or other means of ending one's life.

Vulnerable groups like LGBTQ+ in a hostile environment.

SUGGESTIONS:

People should not ignore a suicide attempt or threat to commit suicide.

In homes, parents should keep medicine and guns away from children and teenagers in a locked place.

We must support one another and encourage our loved ones to seek treatment if we notice any vulnerability.

Also, people should avoid stigmatising mental health issues so that individuals can come out and seek help without appearing weak.

Professionals should provide therapy and early treatment.

The government needs to create awareness of where people can seek assistance or call for help when they are in their units.

CHAPTER 5

SELF CARE

MINDFULNESS

Mindfulness is being present in the moment while non-judgmentally observing one's thoughts and emotions. It means being aware without judging ourselves or others. It helps people not to dwell on the past or worry about the future. Mindfulness can be practised during everyday activities like eating, walking, etc., or during meditation practice. When the mind is occupied, it is not focused on the present. The mind works to think, analyse, and look for problems and solutions. If left alone, the mind will always seek new things to think about and be constantly occupied. It will not be able to focus entirely on the present moment.

Mindfulness is a way to guide the mind to be fully aware and focused on the present moment. By constant practice with determination and patience, we can train the mind to be quiet and fully present in the moment.

Mindfulness helps reduce stress by allowing us to focus

on the present moment. It prevents constant rumination, negative self-talk, and catastrophising. All these amount to stress on the body, so, their reduction will bring peace to the mind and lower our stress levels. It helps lower emotional reactions to situations. Being mindful will help you look at the situation critically without being judgmental, and ushering stress. This is one of the main benefits of mindfulness. It allows us to be focused on the moment, so, we can channel that focus to anything we are doing now without distraction. Distraction is one of the significant causes of stress, so less distraction leads to less stress and more focus.

Mindfulness will help us handle problems in relationships without a judgmental attitude. We can look at the issue without judgment, which can sometimes distort reality.

The use of mindfulness in people with existing mental health challenges needs to be closely monitored by their therapist.

Mindfulness helps reduce symptoms of anxiety and depression as it will help them avoid dwelling on stressful or negative thoughts that will worsen their situation.

Incorporating mindfulness into our everyday lives will bring peace and joy and help us enjoy every moment fully. When we eat, we focus entirely on the food, the taste, the smell, etc. This will also help us avoid overeating or being prone to eating disorders.

Walking: We enjoy every step and appreciate the environment, the sights, and the sounds around us. This will help us enjoy life fully and reduce most of the stress in our lives.

Mindfulness practice is not easy, but with commitment and compassion, we can gradually incorporate it into our lives for an enjoyable experience.

It will help to focus entirely on one thing at a time. Avoid multitasking as much as possible, except when doing work that does not require brain power. If you find your mind wandering, do not be harsh on yourself; bring it back to the present moment.

LETTING GO/NON-ATTACHMENT

Letting go means stopping our attachments to situations, expectations, and desires so we can attain inner peace and accept whatever happens. It encompasses letting go of all worldly wants and desires and our egos. Attachments are standard parts of life, like cravings, but they are at the root of our suffering. So, when we remain attached to people and situations that are unhealthy for us, the attachment will make us suffer.

Letting go is the best way to be happy and have joy in our lives. We must let go of everything that limits us. This includes positive things that we attach so much importance to that losing them will affect our peace.

Letting go ensures we are not so fully attached to anything, be it people, possessions, achievements, or titles, that the loss will destroy our peace. It will help us enjoy life fully, knowing that life is unpredictable. So even if we lose our loved ones or jobs, we can forge ahead, which will be very difficult if we are too attached to them.

Some of the things we need to let go of are:

Judging people (accept people for who they are).

Expectation: it makes us react positively or negatively if what we expect doesn't happen.

The past and future.

GOALS: PROCESS AND OUTCOME

Goals are critical in life. Successful people get to where they are because of the apparent goals they have in mind. Goals are vital in all areas of life, be it business, school, work, sports, or life in general. There are two different types of goals: outcome and process goals.

The outcome goal is focused on what you want to achieve rather than how you intend to achieve it. Outcome goals are outside your control, depending on the type of achievement targeted. For example, if you aim to raise a certain amount of money, which is the target, there is no guarantee you will meet the actual target. So, this can make you frustrated and discouraged. The outcome is the destination you are heading to, and there is no guarantee you will reach that destination. Outcome goals will help you to create a plan towards achieving the actual goal.

Process goals are concrete goals that can be controlled. It is a detailed plan that includes actions to reach the targeted goals. It helps you define the steps necessary to achieve the targeted outcome. Process goals are realistic and specific, e.g., if you want to raise a targeted amount of money at the end of the year, you can make it specific by focusing on monthly targets. Process goals help in habit forming, which helps reach the desired outcome. Process goals are adjustable compared to outcome goals. Also, you have more control over the process goal. A process goal is measured on a step-by-step basis, so it has a shorter time to accomplish than the outcome, e.g., a weightlifter that wants to lift a 100kg weight (which is the outcome) can break the practice into gradual lifting from 50kg to 60kg and gradually to 100kg. This shorter goal will enable him not to feel frustrated by trying to lift 100kg at once.

Focusing on the outcome goal alone can kill motivation, as it is usually a longer-term goal achievable over a long period. However, process goals will fit into your daily activities. You will be motivated to measure your performance and progress towards a more significant outcome. Also, the process goal is a constant reminder of the outcome. Additionally, process goals will help you feel rewarded and push you further to more significant outcome goals. There is a need to put the process and outcome goals in mind. However, be mindful of the fact that process goals have a substantial impact on accomplishing your overall goals.

COMPASSION

Compassion is a strong feeling of another person's pain and involves a desire to help that person.

There are two types of compassion:

Self-compassion: When you treat yourself with kindness instead of criticising yourself or talking to yourself negatively about a mistake you made, you show understanding by accepting that it is okay to make mistakes.

Compassion for others: When you feel other's pain and try to find a way to help them.

Some of the things an individual can do to show compassion:

Apologise to people when you mess up.

Do not talk harshly to people.

Never jump the queue.

Show appreciation and gratitude.

Offer help to people.

Give people a listening ear, and never make assumptions.

Congratulate people on their achievements.

Be kind to yourself and others.

Do not judge people and try to be in their shoes.

Compassion helps in resolving conflict.

It helps remove aggression and defensive attitude during conflict resolution.

It makes people feel at peace; it also reduces stress levels.

It helps boost self-esteem as assisting others makes the

helper feel good about themselves and happier.

It improves our overall mental health.

By being compassionate with ourselves, we tend to be mindful of our behaviour and thought processes.

It helps us form healthy relationships and attracts other people to us.

Compassion helps make the world a better place for all.

WORK-LIFE BALANCE

Work-life balance is how you manage your work-life and other essential things so you can accomplish each goal simultaneously. Apart from work, other essential engagements include family, social life, sports, and spiritual obligations. You have an excellent work-life balance if you can balance all those, successfully. Work-life imbalance will result when no defined and clear-cut boundaries exist between work and other endeavours. Many people struggle to maintain their work-life balance.

Some of the causes of work-life imbalance are:

Perfectionism: Trying to be perfect in your work can lead to excessive time on tasks, which can affect other areas of life.

Fear of losing a job can make the individual overwork.

Technology – using technology, email, etc., can affect work-life boundaries.

Lack of clear-cut boundaries between work and personal life.

Heavy workload and lack of support from superiors.

People who are very ambitious about reaching the top, or making money can spend more time on their work and this deters them from living a busy social life.

Some of the signs of work-life imbalance:

It increases the stress level of the individual. If it becomes chronic, the person can find it difficult to control their emotion, which will impact their mental health.

It affects their productivity at work due to the effect of stress.

It can cause burnout, affecting their mental health, focus, and productivity.

It can lead to poor sleep, which will result in irritability.

SUGGESTIONS:

People must have clear boundaries in everything they do and try to enforce them as much as possible. There should be time for work and time for activities.

They need to focus on essential tasks and manage their time well.

They must communicate with their colleagues, friends, and family and seek support when needed.

The employer must also prioritise workers' welfare. A well-balanced worker will be more productive than a stressed-out worker.

Individuals need to have clear goals for what they want in their work environment and their personal lives.

Practise self-care.

HABIT

Habit is something we do often and regularly without knowing that we are doing it. Habits can be good or bad. They are very hard to break. Bad habits hurt us, but good habits improve our health and well-being. Our brain must crave something for it to be a habit. Our daily actions and behaviour are turned into habits by our brains. The first time we do something, it requires willpower and concentration. But as we repeat it, it becomes easier. The mental energy used to perform it becomes less.

To change a habit, we need to know the trigger (which

tells the brain which habit to use, and when), the routine (emotion/behaviour), and the reward (which is beneficial).

The trigger and reward are significant, which is why we crave something. To change a harmful habit, we need to change the routine to something that is rewarding. It is easier to change an unhealthy habit and replace it with a positive habit by changing the routine action with something else. The reward may include a feeling of relaxation, escape, or distraction.

Trigger – check what you are doing or feeling.

What reward are you after?

Routine: Behaviour you want to change.

Changing a habit requires steady repetition and reinforcement. Good habits make us more efficient, contribute to our overall health and wellness, help us achieve goals, reduce stress, and develop skills. To start a new habit, we need to make a decision, be deliberate about it, and pursue it with determination and compassion. This is because changing negative habits is difficult.

ROUTINE

Routine is something we do in the same way at the same time or place.

Routines are used to organise our time and activities. They help us establish healthy habits and are necessary when we feel uncertain about some aspects of our lives. Routines are essential for our mental health.

It helps us to be productive and focused and form good daily habits.

It helps lower our stress levels and helps us care for our health.

It helps us structure our day and know what to do at each moment.

It helps create independence by making us rely on ourselves instead of others.

It helps provide a way and means to achieve our goals.

SELF-TALK

Self-talk is the way we talk to ourselves. It is our inner voice. It is something we do naturally during the day. It can be positive, which is good for our health, or negative, which adversely affects us. With consistent practice, many who engage in negative self-talk can cultivate positive self-talk.

Negative self-talk is a mean and harsh thought that goes through our heads when we judge ourselves.

Self-talk may help us be present, but it can be very harmful when it becomes excessive.

Effects of negative self-talk:

It limits self-confidence and makes you believe you are not good enough.

It affects your potential to be joyful.

It holds you back from doing certain things, fuelled by the fear of failure.

It leads to self-blame, magnifying minor mistakes into a big disaster.

Adverse childhood experiences, such as parenting styles and behaviours, can significantly contribute to the development of negative self-perceptions. Children who feel consistently abandoned or heavily criticised by their parents may internalise feelings of inadequacy, believing they are not good enough to accomplish certain tasks. These deeply ingrained patterns can persist into adulthood.

Undue high expectations can lead to negative self-talk when a person fails to achieve an expected goal. This can cause them to blame or start criticising themselves unnecessarily for the failure, which can put them in a stressful situation. Not meeting up to peer pressure or some family commitments can also lead to harsh self-blaming.

People who compare themselves unduly with others in terms of success, wealth, and appearance are more prone to engage in negative self-talk when they cannot always meet up.

Moreover, individuals who experience defeat in a competition may excessively self-blame, leading to severe emotional consequences.

Failure - failure in all its forms - is one of the many triggers of negative self-talk in people who are prone to being critical of themselves.

People who are insecure and feel inadequate in certain situations are more at risk.

Some of the risks of negative self-talk:

It will lead to increased stress and put someone at risk of mental health problems due to constant ruminations.

It will limit your productivity and ability to think clearly.

It can worsen depression.

To stop the pattern of negative self-talk: People need to be aware of what they are thinking, so, you can stop that thought pattern and switch to positive ones.

People must change their views about events by accepting that mistakes and failures are part of growth. This will motivate them to learn where they went wrong and how to improve.

People need a therapist whenever it is challenging to handle the thought pattern.

People need to practise mindfulness and always be grateful for all they do.

They need to use positive affirmations.

The more positively they use them, the more their brains will be accustomed to thinking in a positive direction instead of focusing on negatives.

If they find themselves involved in a negative thought pattern, they need to practise self-compassion.

They should not berate or be angry with themselves; they should simply switch to positive self-thought patterns.

Positive self-talk gives people a more optimistic outlook in life.

It helps in stress reduction.

It helps in overall physical health and immune function.

It helps increase productivity.

It makes us appreciate life more.

There is a need for people to be aware of what they are thinking, and make sure it is positive and healthy.

They should be aware of their emotions and know how to respond in a positive and healthy way.

They should focus on solutions and use positive thought patterns to handle challenges.

They should understand that life is unpredictable, do their best, and accept whatever the outcome.

If it is positive, it is okay. If it is negative, they take it and learn how to improve on it next time—always using adverse outcomes as a lesson for improvement.

EXPECTATION

Expectations are what will happen in the future. It can play a role in what will happen and help in the goal and direction to achieve the outcome, but it is not rooted in reality, as nothing is guaranteed. Expectations can be from our thinking process, how we are brought up, or how we learn to see life and cope with it. Expectations make us focus on the outcomes more than the process. People tend to have a visualised idea of how things will turn out and what they expect from the situation. They get frustrated and angry with themselves when their expectations are not met. Also, anger is channelled to others who wish to behave in a certain way. They refuse to see the reality that the outcome of the situation, and the way others behave is not within their control.

Expectation: Expectation is not reality. It is the failure to face and accept the reality of the world we live in. Refusing reality is a source of stress for many people. No one can control reality. It is what it is.

Expectations can make people not appreciate or accept the situation's outcomes. If things turn out as they expected they will be happy, but if the reverse is the case, it will affect their happiness. So, expectations can lower one's sense of gratitude and happiness. Expectations can help us only if we understand the limitations and are grateful to accept any outcome.

People must understand that life is not always fair and that not everyone will like them, no matter how nice they are. They also need to be aware that in life, one can make perfect plans, work with all of one's strength, and may still not accomplish one's objective. Bad things can happen to good people, and good things can also happen to bad people. Nothing is guaranteed in life. Sometimes things won't turn out the way we want them to.

GROWTH MINDSET

A growth mindset is rooted in the belief that we can develop good skills and improve our abilities, talent, and intelligence through hard work and the proper methods. It can benefit everybody. Someone with a fixed mindset believes that skills and talent are fixed from birth and may take time to improve. It is beneficial to switch from a fixed mindset to a growth mindset. This will give us opportunities to learn, improve, and be better at everything we do, with effort and determination.

The many benefits of a growth mindset are:

It helps with productivity and improves everything we do.

It encourages feedback, whether positive or negative, and it is used as the foundation for improvement.

It reminds us that we are not perfect, we can do a lot to improve on it and are willing to be better in all areas of our lives.

It helps us overcome setbacks and fear, endure difficult moments owing to what happened during those periods, and use them as learning tools to turn out better, enabling us to pay less attention to our past mistakes, whilst we continue to improve on anything we do. Thus, our past mistakes serve as the foundation for a better and stronger future.

It leads to less stress as we are not focused on our limitations, mistakes, or bad opportunities in life. We concentrate on making the best of any situation, which enhances our mental well-being.

People reflect on their progress and look for areas of improvement.

They accept mistakes as part of the learning process.

They set realistic goals and practise self-compassion.

They love learning new skills and experimenting with methods to know what works.

People need to examine their thoughts to identify their own mindset. Then, if they notice a growth mindset, they can learn from it, work towards adopting a growth mindset, and if they succeed, apply such strategies in their lives.

A growth mindset accepts uncertainty and changes.

SELF REFLECTION

Self-reflection is the process of profoundly thinking and evaluating our thoughts, feelings, and behaviour. It helps in our self-development; it is part of being a human being and is essential in all our lives. Self-reflection also helps ensure that our values influence our actions. With self-reflection, we are fully aware of how we think, feel, and behave. We need to create time and space for self-reflection so we can observe and check our thoughts nonjudgmentally.

However, self-reflection can be unhealthy if not properly guided and can turn into self-judgment, rumination, negative self-talk, and self-criticism. This will increase our stress levels and impact our mental health. Self-reflection helps us notice things that are healthy or not in our lives and is the reason we can do what is right.

Some of the advantages of self-reflection are:

It is vital to learning.

It helps us analyse what is working and what is not, and the reasons we can act.

It helps us establish healthy boundaries that will enhance our lives.

We can determine what we are willing to accept and what we are not.

It helps us gain a greater understanding of ourselves, knowing who we are, our choices, and what we value.

It brings a fresh idea to some circumstances we are facing.

Self-reflection helps us have good relationships with family, friends, and colleagues.

People need to dedicate time to self-reflection in their daily lives. In those moments, we need to look at our lives and any situation we may encounter. They will help us reflect on what happened, how it made us feel, and how we can improve on the good things in our lives.

Doing this nonjudgmentally with compassion is essential to avoid moving into unhealthy areas when we are involved in negative self-talk.

It takes discipline and constant practice to incorporate it into our lives.

Before self-reflection, we must have a purpose for what we want to know. We should focus on a particular goal to avoid our minds wandering from one issue to another.

Practising gratitude and meditation can help us during the self-reflection journey. It is something to be taken seriously and be intentional about.

HOLISTIC SELF-CARE

A holistic approach to self-care involves activities taken to maintain and support our physical, emotional, social, intellectual, and spiritual well-being and health. To achieve enduring happiness and peace, we need to strengthen all aspects of our lives: physical, emotional, social, intellectual, and spiritual.

For proper functioning in life, we need to have a proper balance and understand the spirit, mind, and body connection. If they are not in alignment, we tend to have problems.

The spirit, in this context, covers our spiritual values, moral beliefs, etc. It is the control centre of our existence. When the mind and body are in alignment with our spirit, we achieve a sense of peace, harmony, and joy in our lives. Each of the three areas needs to be improved upon as any problem with our body, like sickness or disability, will have an impact on our mind. Stress and pressure have a physiological effect on us. Any action that does not agree with our spirit tends to create stress and problems for us. Instead of looking at the solution from our spirit, we tend to look for short-term solutions to the problem. This always leads us to some unhealthy behaviours.

Being spiritually strong means living to our highest self or moral values and being in touch with our creator. That source is always free from negativity or any bad energy. It is always tranquil and full of compassion, love, wisdom, and all positive attributes. When we deviate from the truth, we operate only from our mind. The mind is always chaotic, filled with different thoughts and experiences that we acquire from the world and our environment. This can lead us to behave in a complicated way. We can love and hate, be happy and sad, and all other positive and negative emotions. When we operate from our mind instead of our spirit, we tend to live a complicated life full of stress.

Good things can make us happy, and bad events can make us sad. Those sad moments, if not properly channelled, will have a devastating effect on our mental health. The mind, if properly guided, will lead us to function well in life but not to the optimal level when our spirit is in control of it, so, it pays us to ensure that our spirit controls our mind and body. If we operate from the spirit, we can observe the thoughts in our mind and any challenge in our body without being affected. We can be sick in the body, which affects our mind through the pains and suffering we are passing through. The stresses in our minds can affect our bodies, creating some challenges for our health. The stress can lead to cardiovascular disease and immune problems in the body. We can observe all these without affecting our peace and joy and be detached from those mental and physical challenges. We can look on with compassion at the thoughts going on in our minds without engaging them.

So, the essence of a joyful and peaceful life is ensuring

we can observe our thoughts (mind) and body as observers and witnesses. We observe everything in our world, whether painful or pleasurable, with full awareness, and it will not affect our peace and joy. This is the practice we all need to aim for proper alignment of our spirit, mind, and body to have a more prosperous and joyful life. It takes discipline/commitment to accomplish.

The alignment of the spirit, mind, and body will bring much meaning to our existence. In our social life, we do not need to look for love in anyone to feel good. We know that love lies within us, and from that, it can spread to our mind, making us have compassion for ourselves too, and from there to others. Being compassionate and radiating that love from our spirit will enhance our relationships with people, family, friends, colleagues, etc. If we encounter any bad behaviour from anyone, we do not allow our minds to respond using some thought pattern that may be negative. We enable our spirit filled with compassion to reign. We just look at the person with compassion and, using wisdom (which is part of the spirit's attribute), we respond positively.

Compassion, love, and empathy will embrace all we meet, which will also attract the same to us from people that we encounter. So, in social settings, people's behaviours do not affect how we react. We already know who we are and how to respond.

In our emotional lives, we do not react impulsively to emotions anymore. We observe how we feel, analyse what causes it and why, and look for positive responses. This helps us refrain from judging people because nonjudgmental behaviour is part of our spirit. We can observe our thoughts as a witness but decide based on our spirit/moral system. This helps us to avoid some behaviours linked to our thought patterns, like addiction, cravings, unhealthy habits, etc.

When not attached to a particular thought/feeling, we can observe and know if a behaviour is good. Also, it is essential to know if a specific action aligns with our spirit, so, the need to be addicted to certain things will not be necessary. Therefore, before we take action, it must be aligned with our spirit/morals, and we are aware of the purpose and value. Even when it is pleasurable or bitter, we will know the reason, value, and how to engage. So, the essence of taking a drug/alcohol because it makes us high will not be there because we will only use it for a particular reason.

Also, it helps us to be aware of the dangers of addiction. We get to learn how our brain's reward system operates by releasing feel-good chemicals that make us feel good after pleasurable activities. We are fully aware of how it prevents us from avoiding certain things that will benefit us, but we realise that too much of anything is bad for our health. So, even if sex is sweet and exercise or food is lovely, it does not mean we have to go after it without moderation or control. We know that sweet things can also be dangerous, and some bitter things will be healthy and good for us, and we act accordingly.

It helps us to be very focused and productive in our intellectual lives. There is nothing like distraction in our spirit; focus is the default. So, we can tackle any challenge with focus and guide our minds to avoid unnecessary distractions. This will help end the what-if and why of the mind.

In our physical world, it helps us to ensure that unhealthy habits of the mind that may interfere with the functioning of the physical body are not allowed to thrive. The mind does what the spirit/morals want, so compassion is extended, and the person will know that healthy habits are good for his body, which is equally good for his mind, and adhere to the instructions from his spirit/morals.

We will ensure that we take care of our physical body.

We will ensure our mental health is free from negativity and unresolved trauma.

We will also focus only on what we can control by adopting a healthy lifestyle.

We will ensure that all areas are in top shape to gain the full benefits of healthy living.

Some of the activities that can help us are:

Practising mindfulness/meditation.

Volunteering for a worthy cause.

Healthy living.

Being physically active.

Reducing screen time.

Adequate sleep.

Avoid distraction and negative self-talk.

Stay socially active.

Be mentally active.

Self-reflection.

Good work-life balance.

Frequent medical check-ups.

Always being thankful.

Praying and reading spiritual books.

Nature walks.

Travelling, journaling, and listening to music.

Practise total self-care.

In acceptance of reality, the essence of the spirit, mind, and body alignment cannot be ignored. Acceptance is rooted in accepting reality as it is without the mental/emotional resistance we create in our minds to try to make sense of our world. This resistance is in the form of our choices, how we judge things, and the stories we create to help us make sense of the world. So, we must contend with many things:

our likes and dislikes, wants and rejects, our opinions about people, places, and views about life and the stories we made up. All these emanate from the mind and tend to colour our realities if we hold on so tightly. Our views about people can make us stigmatise or avoid people.

Also, our wants and dislikes are based on our experiences. These tend to affect the way we relate to the world. We may love some and hate others. We may like some things and hate others too.

All these do not have a place where the spirit is entirely in control, as we can focus on the present moment without judgment or bias, but with compassion. This is the main reason for letting go, which is the path to happiness and freedom. This means we are focused on the present moment, without any resistance, and are one with life. Reality is happening now before us, not what we imagined through our thoughts processes. So, when our mind and body are directly under the control of our spirit, we are one with life. We accept whatever outcome comes our way. Our only objective is to do our best in all situations and accept any outcome. The next step is to look at how we can improve based on the outcome.

The body is the anchor of the mind. The mind should be focused on what the body is doing, so if the mind is not present at the moment and is somewhere else, it creates stress in the individual because there is a disconnect. It is like pulling the mind apart from where it is supposed to be and moving it to another place where it is not supposed to be. When the mind is entirely focused on the present where the body is, there is no space for thinking about something else. If you are eating, your mind should be focused on eating; that is how it should operate.

However, we tend to divide the mind into two parts due

to false learning. One is present where the body is, and the other is thinking or worrying about something else. This is why many are so stressed; the energy to do the work is depleted faster by divided attention.

Distraction is the enemy of focus, being present, mind and body uniformity. So, there is a need to be disciplined, practise spirit-mind and body connections, and apply them to our daily lives for optimal performance.

Living a life in perfect alignment with a control centre from the spirit will make living a joyous experience because no negativity is allowed. Also, we can focus entirely and observe what we are thinking and feeling, and our world. So, there's no allowance for ruminating or thinking about what others are doing. We focus entirely on succeeding and learning more ways to be the best in our actions. Anything we do will be given complete focus when we need to sort out a problem or do self-reflection. We know there is an allotted time for doing this after we bring our attention fully to the next action.

This way of life will enhance every avenue of our life. If we are doing anything, attention will be focused on the activity, with no distraction or doubt. We will be fully involved - all our senses will be fully involved. This is the optimal way to function. It is not easy, but with determination, we can be as close as we can to that level of functioning in life.

We must always ensure that we are physically, mentally, and spiritually healthy. No area should be neglected, and they must always be aligned properly.

BIBLIOGRAPHY

Ajzen, 1   ©1988 Attitudes, Personality and Behavior. Dorsey Press, Chicago

Anderson, E ©1999 Code of The Street: Decency, Violence and The Moral Life of The Inner City. W.W. Norton. N.Y

Allan, G.A ©1979 A Sociology of Friendship and Kinship. Allen And Unwin, London.

Allport, G.W. and Postman, L.J ©1947 The Psychology of Rumour. Holt, Rinehart and Winston, N.Y

Aronson E ©2012 The Social Animal. Worth Publishers

Aronson E, Wilson T, Akail, R.L ©2007 Social Psychology. Pearson

Asch. S. ©1962 Social Psychology. Prentice-Hall, N.Y.

Baddeley, A.D Working Memory. ©1986, Clarendon Press, Oxford.

Bandura, A Principles of Behavior Modification. ©1969 Holt, Rinehart and Winston NY.

Bandura, A Self efficacy: The Exercise of Control. ©1997 WH. Freeman NY.

Barling, J Employment, Stress and Family Functioning. ©1990, Barling, J Wiley, Chichester.

Baron, R.A., and Richardson, D. ©1994 Human

Aggression. Plenum, N.Y.

Baron R.A Psychology. ©2001 Allyn and Bacon (Pearson co).

Baumrind, D   ©2008 Parenting for Character: Five Experts, Five Practice. Csee

Beatty. J ©1995 Principles of Behavioural Neuroscience. Brown and Benchmark, Dubuque, I.A.

Beck, A.T and Emery, G. Anxiety Disorders and Phobias: A. Cognitive Perspective. ©1985, Basic Books, N.Y.

Beck, A.T ©1967 Depression; Causes and Treatment. University of Pennsylvania Press, Philadelphia.

Beehr, T. Psychological Stress in The Workplace. ©1995, Routledge, London.

Blood, R.O and Wolfe, D.M.   Husbands And Wives. ©1960, Macmillan N.Y.

Bortfeld, H and Bunge, S. A ©2024 Fundamentals of Development Cognitive Neuroscience. Cambridge University Press.

Bourne, PG ©1974 Addiction. Academic Press NY.

Bowlby. J ©1969 Attachment and Loss Vol 1 Attachment. Basic Books, N.Y.

Buss, A.H, ©1995 Personality: Temperament, Social Behavior, and The Self. Allyn And Bacon, Needham Heights, M.A.

Carnegie, D ©1936 How to Win Friends and Influence People. Simon and Schuster, N.Y.

Chaplin, J.P ©1985 Dictionary of Psychology. (2nd ED) Dell Publishing, N.Y.

Chess, S., and Thomas, A. ©1987 Know Your Child. Basic Books, N.Y.

Coon D, Mitterer J, Martini, T ©2021 Introduction to Psychology: Gateway To Mind And Behavior. Cengage Learning.

Cooper, C.L. and Payne, R (Eds) Causes, Coping and Consequences of Stress at Work. ©1988, John Wiley and Sons. Chichester.

Cornell S., and Hartmann, D. ©1998 Ethnicity and Race: Making Identities in a Changing World. Pine Forge Press, Thousand Oaks CA.

Crowne, D. P. ©1979 The Experimental Study of Personality. Lawrence Erlbaum Associates.

Dawkins, R ©1976 The Selfish Gene. Oxford University Press, Oxford.

Dohrenwend, B.P (ed) ©1988 Adversity, Stress and Psychopathology. Oxford University Press, N.Y.

Du Bois, W.E.B. ©1903 The Souls of Black Folk. Penguin, N.Y'

Durkheim, E. Suicide: A Study in Sociology. ©1952, Routledge and Kegan Paul, London.

Durham, W.H ©1991, Coevolution: Genes: Culture and Human Diversity. Stanford University Press, Standard CA.

Duvals, S, and Wicklund, R. ©1972 A Theory of Objective Self-Awareness. Academic Press, N.Y.

Einstein, A ©1954 Ideas and Opinions. Crown. N.Y.

Evans, P., Hucklebridge, F. And Clow, A. Mind, Immunity and Health. ©2000, Free Association Books, London.

Eysenck, H.J. The Structure of Personality. ©1953, Methuen, London.

Ferber, R ©1985 Solve Your Child's Sleep Problems. Simon and Schuster, N.Y.

Festinger, L ©1957 A Theory of Cognitive Dissonance. Stanford University Press, Stanford,

Fisher, H ©2004 Why We Love: The Nature and Chemistry of Romantic Love. Henry Holt, N.Y.

Fletcher, B.C. Work, Stress, Disease and Life Expectancy. ©1991, Wiley and Sons, Chichester.

Ford, C.S. and Beach, F.A. ©1951 Patterns of Sexual Behavior. Harper and Row, N.Y.

Forward, S, Toxic Parents. ©1989 Bantam Books.

Freud, A The Ego and Mechanisms of Defence. ©1946, International Universities Press, N.Y.

Funder, D.C ©2007. The Personality Puzzle. (4th Ed) Norton, N.Y.

Gauvain, M and Cole, M   ©1997 Reading on The Development of Children. (2nd Edition) Edited by WH Freeman And Companies.

Geertz, C. ©1973 The Interpretation of Cultures. Basic Books, N.Y

Giddens, A ©1984 The Constitution of Society. University of California, Berkeley.

Goldstein, A ©1994 Addiction: From Biology to Drug Policy. Freeman, N.Y.

Goleman, D ©1995 Emotional Intelligence. Bantam Books, N.Y.

Gottesman, I.I ©1991 Schizophrenia, The Origins of Madness. Holt, N.Y.

Hall, G.S ©1916 Adolescence. Appleton, N.Y.

Hampson, S.E ©1988 The Construction of Personality: An Introduction. Routledge, London.

Hatfield, E., Cacioppo, J.T and Rapson, R.L ©1994 Emotional Contagion. University of Cambridge Press, Cambridge.

Hare, R.D ©1999 Without Conscience: The Disturbing World of The Psychopaths Among Us. Guilford, N.Y.

Heine, S. J. ©2008 Cultural Psychology. W.W Norton and Companies.

Hochschild, A.R ©1983 The Managed Heart: Commercialization of Human Feeling. University of California Press, California.

Henry, J.P ©1977 Stress, Health and The Environment. Springer – Verlag, N.Y.

Houghton, P and Robinson, D ©2003 Advanced Psychology. Contemporary Press.

Hugdahl, K. ©2001 Psychophysiology: The Mind-Body Perspective Harvard University Press. Cambridge. M.A.

James, W ©1950   The Principles of Psychology Dover N.Y.

Jones, H ©1997 I'm Too Busy to Be Stressed. Hodder And Stoughton, London.

Jones, F and Bright, J   ©2001 Stress: Myth, Theory and Research. Pearson Education Ltd.

Karasek, R.A. and Theorell, T. ©1990 Healthy Work Stress, Productivity and The Reconstruction of Working Life. Basic Books, N.Y.

Kosslyn, S. M, Rosenberg, R.S   ©2005 Fundamentals of Psychology: The Brain, The Person, The World. (2nd Edition) Pearson.

Kremer, J. and Skully, D. ©1994 Psychology in Sport. Taylor And Francis, London.

LeDoux, J.E ©1996 The Emotional Brain: The Mysterious Underpinnings of Emotional Life. Simon and Schuster, N.Y.

Lemme, B.H ©1995 Development in Adulthood. Allyn and Bacon, Needhan Heights M.A.

Livingston B, A ©1985 Stressmanship. Severn House Publishers, London.

Marks, I.M ©1969 Fears and Phobias. Academic Press, N.Y.

Miller, T.W (Ed) ©1989 Stressful Life Events. International Universities Press, Madison CT.

Morgan, C. T, King, R.A, Weisz, J.R, Schopler, J ©1986 Introduction to Psychology. 7th Edition Tata McGraw-Hill.

Myers, David G   ©2001 Psychology. 6th Edition. Worth

Publishers.

Nairne, J. S ©2003 Psychology: The Adaptive Mind. (3rd Edition) Wadsworth (Div of Thomson Learning).

Newton, T ©1995 Managing Stress: Emotion and Power at Work. Sage, London.

Ornstein, R. E. ©1972 The Psychology of Consciousness. (2nd Edition), WH. Freeman and Company.

Parkes, C.M ©1972 Bereavement: Studies Of Grief in Adult Life. Penguin Books, Harmondsworth.

Pinker, S ©1997 How the Mind Works. Norton N.Y.

Piotrkowski, C.S ©1978 Works and The Family System. The Free Press, N.Y.

Rosenberg, M. ©1965 Society and The Adolescent Self Image. Princeton University Press, Princeton N.Y.

Scribner, S., and Cole, M ©1981 The Psychology of Literacy. Harvard University Press, Cambridge N.Y.

Selye, H ©1976 The Stress of Life. (R E) McGraw – Hill, N.Y.

Shafter, D. R ©2002 Developmental Psychology. 16th Edition Wadsworth Group.

Skolnick, A.S. ©1987 The Intimate environment: Exploring Marriage and Family. Little, Brown, Boston.

Streiker, L.D. ©1984 Mind-Bending: Brainwashing, Cults, and Deprogramming in The 80's. Double Day, Garden City N.Y.

Tomasello. M ©1999 The Cultural Origins of Human Cognition. Harvard University Press Cambridge M.N.

Vygotsky, L.S. ©1978 Mind in Society. Harvard University Press, Cambridge.

Warr, P. ©1987 Work, Unemployment and Mental Health. Oxford University Press, Oxford.

Zborowski, M ©1969 People in Pain. Jossey-Bass, San Francisco.

Stress (C) 2024 21february 2023, www.who.int/news.room/questions-and-answers/item/stress

Coping With Stress 21 May 2024, www.cdc.gov/mentalhealth/cope-with-stress/index.html

Mindfulness Meditation, Oct. 30 2019, www.apa.org/mindfulness/meditation

Addiction, my.clevelandclinic.org/health/diseases/6407-addiction (C) 2024

(C) 2017 Parenting Styles-apa.org/act/resources/factsheets/parenting-styles

Nov. 3, 2023, Control anger before it controls you, apa.org/topics/anger/control

Anxiety disorders 27 Sept. 2023 (C) 2024 who who.int/news-room/fact-sheets/detail/anxiety disorders

©2024 Depressive Disorder (Depression) 31 March 2023 who.int/newsroom/factsheet/detail/depression

Effects of Bullying May 21, 2021, stopbullying.gov/b

INDEX

Made in the USA
Monee, IL
07 July 2026

56553661R00085